Softcover ISBN: 978-1-7352547-2-2
Ebook ISBN: 978-1-7352547-0-8
Kindle Mobi ISBN: 978-1-7352547-1-5

1st Edition August 1st, 2020

Contents

Dedication

Steven

I am well aware that I am only who I am and where I am due to every single person in my life. Every interaction—positive or negative—has made me who I am. For all of those who've touched a part of my life, my gratitude knows no bounds.

To my incredible wife, Katalin for keeping me on point and making me a father, my children, Maximilian and Csenge for their constant inspiration, my strong mother, Sandra who greatly influenced my path, my father, Stanley who is my best friend, my brother, Scott for the undying support, my sister, Shelley because she just gets me, Command Sergeant Major Alton B. Eckert who was beside me in battle and taught me what leadership in battle really is, as well as my friends, adversaries, teams, and the leaders who took the time to give me a chance to be the greatest version of myself, I say: "Thank you for contributing to who I am. I am truly humbled."

Lane

I am grateful to all of those who have helped me on my journey. Every step of the way, a leader, mentor, or friend helped guide me in the right direction. Thank you to my family and close friends for shaping me, even when you didn't realize you were doing so.

Best Mom—thank you for showing me how to love; My wife, Ali, thank you for showing me how to become the person I'm supposed to be. Thank you, Kris, for bringing me in like a brother; Kenny, for helping me remain thoughtful; Ben, for being a shining light of positivity; A.J., for inspiring strength; and Ronnie, for guidance in dangerous places. Thank you to the countless others for sparking ideas, providing feedback, and for simply being my friend.

Foreword

"The Difference Between Management and Leadership
is Communication"

—Winston Churchill

As a young leader, I learned to yell to get a person's attention. As an old leader, I know the power a properly placed whisper has to capture attention.

For over 30 years, I've had the joy of being in business in a variety of capacities and have worked inside 300+ corporations including Johnson & Johnson and Samsung, as well as start-ups like GoPro, Eagle One, and Oxi-Clean. I've seen how the big boys do it and how the little guys grow it. There aren't many folks who have been paid to get this kind of education, and it has been nothing short of humbling and awe-inspiring.

I've had the distinct privilege to see humans ascend and lead with honor. I've seen some real idiots, too. I'm always flabbergasted by the amazing incompetence of some people who rise to power. Quality leadership has no age, color, sex, and is definitely not an inherited trait. If anything, it skips two or three generations (successful entrepreneurs often raise spoiled, entitled children, but that's a lesson for another day).

When you think about great leaders, men like Winston Churchill, Abraham Lincoln, Henry Ford, Dr. Martin Luther King, and even today's business moguls like Bill Gates, Steve Jobs, Jeff Bezos, and Elon Musk come to mind. There is also a whole cadre of women who are recognized as great leaders, including Mara Bara, Merillyn Hewson, Sheryl Sandberg, and Indra Nooyi.

As you consider the personalities of these great leaders, it's clear there is no magic formula. Yet, the leaders above all share common traits such as vision, articulation, self-motivation, and team building. Before the world praised these "Hall of Famers," they (and many others I've met) were leading with additional traits such as empathy, intelligence, integrity, and honesty.

So what does it really take to become a leader, and how do you become the type of leader people naturally follow?

Well, for one—most great leaders don't announce themselves. Anyone who foolishly tells you how great he is and how much his team loves him is—more often than not—a tyrant the moment you walk away. The self-proclaimed messiah usually turns out to be someone the entire team wishes permanent influenza on.

We often think that leadership is about knowing what to say and how to say it. My experience is that great leaders develop a high level of confidence and intuition. They also know when to stop talking and let the silence do the work.

Leadership results in admiration, comradery, and love. And a true leader should be humbled by those outpourings. A leader doesn't work in order to receive love, however. It's a by-product of fulfilling his mission and serving his team well. Being a great leader is not universally equated with being a nice person whom everyone loves. In fact, if you see a nice and loveable person in a top leadership role, that's usually a sign of a soft organization where the top dog is a lapdog to the staff. It's fair to say that our favorite leaders are not always nice, yet they are kind. They are not arrogant, yet they embody and spread confidence. They are not soft, yet they possess compassion.

The recipe for leadership includes ingredients like drive, intention, maturity, wisdom, passion, compassion, humility, bravery, emotional intelligence, and intellect. It's quite an ingredient list, but it can be summed up in one word: character. All great leaders have character.

Like I said before, these qualities aren't really inherited. They surface either from your own adversity, or from so deeply empathizing with the adversity of others you want to lead them out. You cannot take a person with excellent skills who lacks character and turn him into a great leader. Yet, you can take a person with great character and almost no skills and cultivate an amazing leader.

Most of the people that we regard throughout history as great leaders paired accomplishment with a sense of humanity, innovation, and perseverance inside a moral construct of being a good human. Some of them, however, had awful relationships with their family members, partners, and sometimes even with their employees and customers. Even though their character may come into question in one area of their life or another, the people that history esteems all possess a collective set of values that deliver results for the greater good.

Considering all of that, can you really become a great leader and have it all? Certainly. First, you have to decide whether you want to <u>have it all</u>.

So, first rule: Don't be a tool. Get a tool box.

This book is a treasure trove of tools and is set up to be a virtual mentor for you. It's a guide to help you map out your ascension to mature and wise leadership. It is not a "self-help" or "fix it" guide. By following the path the authors lay in front of you, you will develop the characteristics and habits necessary to accelerate your growth and into profound leadership. You'll feel the shift and others will notice it.

Learning leadership skills from a couple of ex-soldiers might, at first glance, seem counterintuitive. You might think you're in for a lesson solely on discipline, structure, and execution. Far from it. Understand that the door of the military swings wide open for recruits from all walks of life. Officers are often educated and come from highly academic universities and military academies such as Annapolis and West Point.

There is no one "military person." This book is not authored by officers. Its creators were enlisted men who rose to high levels of leadership from the ground up. Picture the world these guys came from as combat soldiers: Imagine sitting in an armoured vehicle in the middle of a fire zone in 113 degrees in a uniform that's even hotter. You see glimpses of fear in everyone's eyes, noise penetrates your ears, and chaos threatens to cloud your mind.

Just like a soldier, your life and work has a microcosm of similar stressors. In a world of employment lawsuits and HR departments, emotionally intelligent superstars and non-committed nitwits, relationship struggles and inner conflict, a leader navigates and adapts just like a seasoned soldier.

As I did in my own leadership journey, you can ascend and overcome by being observant, taking action, remaining humble, and always being willing to take the risk of being humiliated.

How do you do it without being a threat to the monkeys on the rungs of the ladder above you? How should you navigate office politics and games? In this book, you'll learn how to sidestep the nonsense and be the individual that is noticed and respected. You'll become the dignified bull with no bullshit.

This book is about you becoming the natural leader you already are inside. It has nothing to do with learning how to manipulate others and everything to do with learning how to step into profound leadership.

Leadership, in its essence, is the work of the Almighty. It is you living out your God-given powers of creation to manifest phenomenal Quality of Life for you, and impact for others. Whether you bought this book for yourself or were given it after someone else read it and was impacted, I recommend you follow it. Take it to heart.

You possess the divine gift of leadership. My prayer is that you find the joy of stripping away anything that is slowing your rise in your business, relationships, and God-given talents so you can bring out the very best in yourself and everyone you touch.

From the battlefield to the boardroom, Steven and Lane have cultivated the level of leadership that drives results, develops tight-knit teams, unlocks purpose, and strengthens relationships. They have discovered a massive power within themselves and can show you how to tap into it, too. The hundreds of people they have guided are proof of that.

Ron Lynch
Business Strategist
Direct Consumer Acquisition Agency - Principal
4 Billion in Direct to Consumer Revenue

Preface

Around 1991, after a ceasefire in Iraq during Operation Desert Storm, we set up a post near Basra. We were about 100 kilometres into Iraq in a buffer zone around Kuwait. It was a checkpoint where we processed, fed, and held enemy prisoners of war. While we were there, however, scared and hungry civilians came to us in droves for food and safety, and we couldn't help them because they weren't military combatants.

I remember fathers—with their wife and children by their side—on their knees, hugging my legs and begging for assistance; for us to let them into our no-fire zone and help them. These were women, children, and families, and to be forced to turn people away from help was gut wrenching. I had to block out what was happening in front of me or I would have completely broken down. You know those moments when you're forced to—heck, you're trained to—push all emotion aside, stay focused, and drive forward? These were those moments. I vividly remember having to ignore my feelings—my humanity—and I did it. I was good at it, because what else do you do? This is how you advance in the military.

Some people may remember that during that time, President George Bush Senior told the Shiites that if they formed an uprising, our troops would come and help them fight. For two days, we battled the Iraqi Republican Guard from the Al-Madinah and Tawakalna Divisions at the now famous Battle of 73 Easting, the largest tank battle since the Second World War, and after that the Shiites rose up, but we were told to stand down. They were massacred and started flooding our checkpoint with refugees.

One day, I was standing at Checkpoint Charlie, looking across the desert and I saw a little pink dot. I stood there staring, thinking *What the hell is that?* As it got a little closer, I saw that it was a little girl with both of her arms stretched straight out to the side. I thought she was playing airplane, but as she walked closer and closer, I saw that her arms were outstretched because burns covered her body. She wore a pink summer dress over the clothes that were burned into her skin.

Still pushing my emotions away, I took her in and led her to the medic tent. What I saw was killing me, but I kept trying to keep it together. As I tried to push what I was feeling down, I realized that I just had to stop. I needed to feel, to allow the gravity of the situation to wash over me and process what was really happening rather than push it down. I knew at that moment that rather than put a wall up, I needed to find a way to connect with this little girl—to see the reality of what (and who) was in front of me.

There wasn't much I could do. I wasn't able to control the situation and help her the way I wanted to. I wanted to pick her up and hug her. I wanted to take her somewhere safe, feed her, give her shelter, and ensure that she could grow up to be a fabulous and amazing woman; but that was impossible. Most people might stop there and think that, because of the lack of control and limits, they can only say hello and goodbye or do nothing at all. But, I knew I could do something, even if it was a smidgen of goodness and kindness. Instead of accepting that I couldn't help her in the way that I wanted, so I couldn't help her at all, I accepted that I could do even the smallest act.

I had to be comfortable with the fact that I had no control over the situation. I couldn't transform this little girl's life; I couldn't stop the war. We run into these situations in business and in life. Sometimes people are blocking us or something isn't working. A lot of people think, *Well, I have no control so there's nothing I can do.* This is the pivotal moment where leaders rise. At times, leaders must accept that they don't have control, but understand that they can always add value, insight, or kindness to change the world that's in front of them. They may not be able to change the larger world or situation, but they can change the course of a small moment in time or a thought in a person's mind.

At that moment, pain, fear, and heartache rushed over me. I recognized my humanity and the fact that there was so much I wanted to change, but I could only change small moments within our brief encounter.

My Aunt "Boots" (which is what we called her) sent me butterscotch candy while I was deployed. I kept pieces in my uniform pocket and as the little girl walked out of the medic tent, I got down on one knee, pulled a butterscotch candy out, and handed it to her. She took it, looked at me, and smiled. I can't even explain what that did to me. It was all I could do, but it was what I could do. And it's the "what" that matters. At that moment, I like to believe I opened a small door for her to move through even a morsel of her trauma.

I realized that what we were doing over there probably wasn't the best thing for the world. We like to look at our business, career, global warming, or mission in life and say we're going to change the world. And that's noble and good, but we can really only change what's in front of us. We can only change our world—our micro world—and let it ripple from there.

If you're in a career and you realize that you can't change the whole company, realize you can change, influence, and add value and intention to the areas that you're responsible for. You can make a massive difference even if it appears small.

With that little girl, I like to think that I created a moment of love in a situation where it should have been completely impossible. I wanted so badly to control that situation, but I accepted that I couldn't and did what was in my power to add value to the small world—the micro cosmos—around me.

Tears streamed down my face as she walked back out into the desert. I take solace in the fact that maybe she's still alive and that small moment helped her get through the next years of her life. If you're reading this book and you've ever heard that story from a little Iraqi girl who's probably somewhere between 35 to 38 years old at the time of this writing, I'd love to meet her again and tell her how my encounter with her impacted my life.

I realized I had to stop pushing away what was happening around me in order to get ahead and get through. I had to get comfortable having a lack of control to change what I couldn't change and do my best to transfer the good inside of me to others in whatever way I could. As you begin your Humble Alpha journey, I realize that as much as we say "you control your situation" (and you do!), there may be circumstances outside of your control that you cannot change. Remember, leaders rise in impossible situations. They change what's in front of them through moment-by-moment transfers to others of what they carry inside. They end up changing the world by first changing *their* worlds.

~ *Steven Kuhn*

Introduction

Even when I, Steven, was in high school, I hungered for more. In an attempt to satisfy that hunger, I did all of the wrong things. Something inside me knew I was called to greatness, but I was basically a knucklehead. I was the worst at sports, which didn't stop me from trying, but I still loathed myself and was as unlucky in love as Mr. Bean.

I was arrogant because I was insecure. I wanted to travel, meet interesting people, and scale the walls to get out of my self-inflicted prison, but people continuously pulled me down. If it wasn't their words, it was their labels. They had power over me, because I hadn't yet realized the power I had inside me. I was my own worst enemy, and I had a bag full of excuses. And then, something changed.

I realized the difference between the knucklehead and the high-achiever; that guy who stood on the ground, head cocked back, admiring the huge mountain, but going nowhere, was me. The difference was, of course, my self-belief and acceptance; I could stand in my own way or I could get the hell out of it.

I got the hell out of it.

I joined the military, rose through the ranks, went to war, and learned quickly that life was up to me and only me. When I left the military a few years later, I battled an onslaught of PTSD, depression, and a failed marriage. If that wasn't enough, my body was no longer the same. Ravaged by Gulf War Syndrome, every day became an uphill battle as chronic symptoms attacked my muscles, nerves, and organs like the war adversaries we fought to defeat.

Told I'd never be physically healed, I kept searching. I searched for my own internal answers, too. I discovered the healing power of a plant from the Amazon Rainforest and a quiet Benedictine monastery in Austria.

I realized that everything on the outside is a result of what we do on the inside.

It took years of work but I figured out who I was, learned to genuinely love myself, and dug deep into my passions and hobbies.

I identified my life's vision and mission and painted a crystal clear picture of it. I learned to build unbreakable habits and unshakeable routines. I broke every bad habit that plagued my previous life (which is, of course, a continuous, life-long process of change)

I lived all over the world and traveled extensively, turning around million-dollar companies that were on the brink of disaster. I learned how to get exactly what I want out of life. The harder the task, the more challenging the situation, the more resolute I am to make it happen because I've never forgotten what I learned: It all comes from within. We decide who we are and what we can create.

Over a 20-year period, I sat at the feet of masters and learned their secrets. I learned how to leverage teams and have massive impact on people and organizations. After 15 years of working with sacred plant medicine from the Amazon, I discovered things about the body and mind and this world most people will go to their grave disbelieving.

I married a perfect woman who continuously shows me she wants me to be happy, even if that means I spend a significant amount of time traveling around the world. Every morning I'm home, I have coffee with her and our small children on our sofa. We're consciously with each other and express the love we have for one another. She never gives me the cold shoulder when I travel or have an unexpected meeting, because she knows it makes me happy; and of course she has a shoulder to lean on when she needs it, as do I. Daily, I'm humbled by the knowledge that our paths would have never crossed—that I would have never met my wife—had I not completely accepted who I am and gone through the stages of unleashing my Humble Alpha.

My kids look to me for their significance and I point them back to themselves. I do my best to highlight the light that flickers within, and teach them how to tap into it. I don't pave the path for them, but I prepare them for the path, so one day I don't have to dig them out of a mess, because they have a shovel and know how to use it.

I unleashed my Humble Alpha; then I started teaching others to do the same.

I've watched men worth multiple millions break down and cry because they didn't know who they were and their wives and kids didn't respect them. I gave them the tools and strategies I'd applied in my own life and watched them unleash their Humble Alpha, too.

Lane joined the military with a lot of drive yet little direction. It was an unexpected door that opened his world to more. Leaders surrounded Lane, guiding his ambition and eventually unveiling his path to become a Green Beret. Becoming a leader in some of the most dangerous and austere places on the planet catapulted him to explore even greater unknowns.

Missions around the world hardened his mentality—thickening his resolve and fortifying his endurance—while exposing him to the untapped secrets and unlimited possibilities this world has to offer. Even in the roughest places on Earth, he could see the kindness and beauty of it. Later, he learned to polish the roughest places in his own character and expose its kindness and beauty, as well.

He knew he was called to greatness, too. He shunned the status quo and pursued meaning and purpose. He chased down answers to life's biggest questions and the world became his playground. He scaled mountains in Peru and meditated in temples, learning to shed his ego and reach deep within.

He shook off the shackles of the world, leaving possessions to quench his unquenchable thirst for adventure. He carried home inside of him, so that it didn't matter where he planted his feet; he had everything he needed within.

He became friends with his intuition and learned what it really looked like to look fear in the face and tell it to move the hell out of the way. He walked through uncertain doors and lassoed his dreams.

He married an incredible woman who shares his thirst for adventure. He grew in wisdom, knowledge, and power. People can't touch him, and yet he's always within reach for those in need.

He unlocked his creativity, blew the lid off of his limitations, and learned to open his mind to a realm of untapped potential and absolute peace.

Nothing can stir or shake him, and yet he's moved by the subtle flitter of a butterfly's wings and the massive power Amazonian plants have on the human body.

He started helping people unlock what he'd discovered. Together, we started helping people.

This book is about how we helped ourselves, and how we help others. It's a journey that walks you step-by-step through how to unleash your Humble Alpha. If you follow what we show you and do what we say, you'll have what we have. You'll activate your true identity, develop hungry teams, and create legendary Quality of Life.

To get the most out of this book, don't rush through it. Read each section and complete the action steps at the end of each one. If you read the book and don't do the work, you won't get what you want—period. You have to dig deep to unleash, because for many of you, what you're looking for has been buried for a very long time.

A Note About the Writing:

> *When reading a co-authored book, it is often hard to tell exactly who is saying what, and this book is no exception. "I" in this book may refer to either Steven or Lane and, of course, "we" refers to both of us.*

WHAT IS A HUMBLE ALPHA?

What's a Humble Alpha? What's the big idea?

A Humble Alpha is proud, but not full of pride.

He's not cocky, and he doesn't puff his chest out to make a point.

He's confident, and he walks with his head held high, never hanging his head down (unless it's to tie his shoe).

The trials and tribulations of this world don't have him on a leash, he unleashes the greatness within himself and others.

He sees the potential in every person, even when others don't.

He believes in abundance, not scarcity, which means he knows there's enough to go around. He won't hand you a smaller piece, so he can get more. He also won't ask you to take a step back so he can step forward and position you in his shadow.

He can tell you who he is, where he comes from, and where he's going.

But, he won't make you feel like less of a person if you don't know those things about yourself.

To him, you belong with his band of brothers.

There isn't a secret handshake, but there are secrets.

And, he's prepared to share them with you—to help you unleash your Humble Alpha.

A Humble Alpha operates from a place of completeness. He's whole, which means he can elevate others rather than make digs at them in an attempt to fill his own void. He pours into others because his cup is full and running over.

He respects free will—honoring every person's choices and unique expressions.

Judgement doesn't occupy space inside of him, which means empathy flows freely and allows him to build harmonious communities that become beacons of light to the world.

His purpose and identity are clearly defined. No matter what his job title says, he positions himself to amplify his vision and mission through his business, projects, hobbies, and every other thing he does in life.

A Humble Alpha has tremendous power inside, and others see it without him saying a word.

His wife respects him, his kids listen to him, and his friends go out of their way to support him.

He's driven and resilient; he transcends plateaus and tears down barriers.

He wields influence and shields the hurting.

No one tells him what to do or who he is.

No one tells him which way to go, and yet he heeds directions.

He always listens and asks questions more than he talks.

He makes people laugh or cry with his stories of the past, but he doesn't live there.

His bag of stories never runs dry, because he never stops living or listening to interesting people whom others overlook.

He's not addicted to applause; and while addictions might scar his past, when he became a Humble Alpha, he rose above them.

He dives deeply and is open to communicating why he acts a certain way and what his triggers are.

He sits with discomfort, embraces it even.

He lives by principles and values, not by peer pressure or trends.

He has no secret motives.

He always speaks the truth, especially when it's hard because he knows a lie always makes him lay down the best part of himself.

He accepts responsibility for his wrongdoings because he knows it's the only way to undo the wrong and to learn from it.

He takes ownership of his current situation and his actions, knowing that only he has the power to change, and only when he takes hold of that power will change actually happen.

He's situationally aware and intuitively knows the next move to make, trusting himself and taking action.

He sees failures as lessons and isn't afraid to fail fast and fall hard.

He always gets up.

A Humble Alpha opens his hand to receive the good and bad that comes his way. He appreciates both for how they bring him to one defining moment after another, making him the man he is.

While he appreciates the hard and dark places, he doesn't dwell there. He makes his bed in the land of the good and focuses on it, knowing by gazing at goodness, he opens his capacity to experience more of it in his life.

He knows what the moment calls for and lives fully present in every one, knowing he creates the best reality when he appreciates, focuses on, and turns his attention towards all that's before him.

Every action a Humble Alpha takes is intentional. Whether he's watching a movie, mapping out a new idea, or making a phone call, he knows why he does what he does and how it adds value to his life and the lives of others.

He's always growing and always mastering.

He trains his body and stays on top of his game.

He eats well, laughs hard, and loves passionately.

He can meditate on the top of a mountain, shake hands with a beggar on the street, and run a board meeting for a multi-million-dollar company.

He dresses to impress, but he doesn't try to impress you or anyone else, for that matter.

He gives whatever it takes, runs towards greatness, and realizes his dreams.

He's the one you see and want to be, and he's the one who tells you never to be anyone but who you are.

The Humble Alpha is you.

Let's unleash him.

THE FIVE STAGES—AN OVERVIEW

We're excited to share our insights about becoming a Humble Alpha with you. We believe that through this book, you'll unleash the power already within. We say "you," because, ultimately, it's up to you. We're here to guide you, equip you, and elevate you so that you can step into your greatness.

We've broken the Humble Alpha journey into five stages, which are laid out in five sections throughout this book. We'll dive into each one in detail throughout the book, but we want you to know that significant thought, experience, and wisdom has gone into the development of these five stages and their order. We don't teach theory; we teach what we've lived and applied to our own lives to become Humble Alphas ™. Many have gone before you; this is the proven process we walk them through.

The five stages to unleashing your Humble Alpha are: Activate, Unleash, Empower, Momentum, and Lebensqualitäte. The first two stages solidify the foundation of your individuality and show you how to reveal your true identity and actual purpose. From that position, you amplify your Humble Alpha outside of yourself. This is where stages three, four, and five come in.

Stage Three focuses on your company or business and unpacks how to empower your team and build an undeniable company culture. Then, everyone around you moves towards unleashing their Humble Alpha. In stage four, we transcend the walls of the organization and show you how to expand the reach of your Humble Alpha throughout the marketplace and world. In stage five, we paint a picture of what real lebensqualitäte (Quality of Life) looks like and show you how to create it. Let's take a look at each stage in more depth.

Activate

We activate credit cards, newsletter subscriptions, and external items but how often do we activate ourselves? When you activate your Humble Alpha, you learn how to let go of your old identity that's keeping you stuck and claim a new one so you never have to struggle with insecurity, bad habits, or a lack of success again. When you activate, you discard your demons because they no longer control you. You turn off the hateful voices in your head and turn on your Humble Alpha.

Unleash

We believe you already possess within you the fortitude to reach your highest level of greatness. We believe the Humble Alpha is simply waiting to be awakened. When you unleash your Humble Alpha, you uncover your real purpose, needs, and vision for your life. You also identify the needs of your company, family, community, or organization because when you align your identity and purpose with your business or those within your reach, you amplify your success and theirs.

Empower

In this stage, we show you how to empower everyone around you. We give you the tools and scripts to release value that boomerangs back and often extends so far you don't even see where it lands. We show you how to stop people from interrupting you with trivial questions and learn how to make excellent decisions on their own from an empowered position in your company. You'll learn proven methods and successful strategies that show you how to create hungry teams who want what you want and align with your mission.

Momentum

Humble Alpha momentum is all about amplifying your influence outside of your organization and in every facet of your life. The concepts we talk about in this section apply to every interaction you have, but to make this easily understandable, we journey through it here because it amplifies every stage before it. You'll learn how to build partnerships and joint ventures that skyrocket your success and amplify your reach so you can move faster and further in the direction of your mission.

Lebensqualitäte

Lebensqualitäte is a German word that means Quality of Life (QOL). We capitalize Quality of Life, because it means something special. We want you to pause for just a moment when you read it and know it's the ultimate endstate; the final "state" to arrive to. It's the goal to continuously move towards and yet it is also part of the journey. By capitalizing it, we want you to know there is emphasis on this being something more than a word that's tossed around. Reflect on whether you truly have Quality of Life

In this stage, you adopt the life principles that a Humble Alpha lives by to have maximum Quality of Life. We discuss concepts like H.I.T.(honesty, integrity, and transparency) and QOL to build a foundation for a life that makes you happy to be alive, keeps you energized and on top of your game, and gets you excited to dominate in every arena.

High Ego vs Humble Alpha

If you're a high-ego guy who powers through the stages and still doesn't know if you want to change and tap into your Humble Alpha, let us warn you—you're walking a tightrope! When you have a falsely inflated ego, you live in danger of being pushed off of your stool. You're one push away from being laid out. Resting in a high-ego is an unstable place to be. Anyone who is a Humble Alpha or a true leader picks up on it immediately and knows you're compensating.

When it comes to your ego, take a look at how it operates in your body, mind, and relationships in business. Here's an example of how your ego works. Let's say you start gaining weight, and your body takes a hit. What fills in the gap? Your ego and this is where it'll get bigger and bigger. Take another example of the CEO who has power at work, but at home has a wife who gives him stress and kids who don't respect him. He stays at work and talks loudly and brash to his team to compensate for what he doesn't have at home. He needs love and self-respect.

In this situation, your ego typically gets in the way and starts creating admiration through fear rather than respect. People respect the position, but not the man in the position. The first step towards change is to realize the ego will not take you where you want to go. You will never reach the highest level in your career or life if it's running the show. Ego can be healthy, and you need your ego, but it's not something that you want to wear on your sleeve.

The old idea of an alpha male is often associated with this kind of guy. The guy who has a chip on his shoulder, the one who compensates and is always brash. To address this association that many have, we tie humility to the alpha. Humility is what allows an alpha to dominate in his life, business, and home organically and from a place of sustained inner power.

The Humble Alpha will take you to the highest level and the highest Quality of Life. Whether you're dealing with an overextended ego, a balanced one, or a deflated one, we can release your inner Humble Alpha.

Section One

ACTIVATE

⌒

"Man conquers the world by conquering himself."

– Zeno of Citium

One cannot freely give, what one does not have. One cannot elevate the world, when one hasn't elevated himself. One cannot provide happiness to the world, when one isn't happy himself. By conquering yourself and becoming a Humble Alpha, you will be able to conquer your world, in the most positive way possible.

It's the small moments in your control that really change the world: moment by moment, choosing growth over fear, choosing humility over pride. Conquering yourself won't happen by accident. You won't slip into greatness. Only by firmly committing to yourself and deciding, will you be able to conquer the world.

We are What We Decide

Who are you?

Take a moment and sit with that question; roll it around in your mind. If you're tempted to answer with, "I'm Joe." Who is Joe? Imagine we're sitting across the table from one another and having a couple of drinks. If I asked you what you want to be and where you want to go, could you answer? Would you choke on your beer? Swallow hard, and then stumble through a half-baked answer? Don't stress—most men can't answer that question, which is why most men never reach the highest level of greatness and achieve the Quality of Life they envy.

Many men want to live differently. They want the respect they deserve and the spontaneous affection they long for. They want a different experience out of life, but they never decide to go after it. Going after it doesn't mean divorcing your wife, quitting your job, or parting ways with the barber you've used since you were 12-years-old. It means you stop being wishy-washy, and stop settling for standing on the sidelines. It means you flip the switch in your mind and decide you are unleashing your Humble Alpha. By picking up this book, you took the first step on the journey to your highest self.

The next step in activating your Humble Alpha is to get clear on what you want to be and where you want to go. You have to do this work. We're your guides, but we won't change your life—you will! A new book or course isn't going to change your life. When you decide you've had enough and you're ready, then you'll change, but not until then.

Identity is who you are and how you show up in the world. Most people don't know who they are. They have inklings, ideas, or brief glimpses, but they pull back from them. Most people take on an external identity based on who their parents said they were or how they think they need to behave to get the treatment they want. In this book, we help you get away from every preconceived notion about who you think you should be and how you think you should show up in the world. Then, we help you hone that identity, so you unleash what already exists deep inside of you.

Real leadership stems from this true identity; it's what allows you to dominate in any space. Perhaps you've seen strong men in powerful leadership positions step out of the office and into a social setting, and all of the sudden act shy and out of place. That happens because they've stepped outside of their power zone. They've allowed their strength and power to come from their title, not their identity. Many people latch onto external things, whether it be accomplishments, accolades, job titles, or degrees. They grasp onto things outside of themselves and say: "This is part of my identity."

We're military guys, but our military experience only partially amplifies our true identity. We were a part of the military, and it helped shape us tremendously, but we're individuals with a unique purpose in life outside of that. We didn't follow the cement path of military life or any other kind of life, for that matter. We paved our own way because an internal compass and solid identity led us to one significant step after another and ultimately to the highest version of ourselves. Transformation is a continual process, which means we keep going higher and higher. You can, too.

The first external thing that people latch onto is always their job title. You aren't your title. If you ask someone who they are, 90-95% of the time, they tie it to a job title or an accomplishment. You hear, *"I'm a consultant,"* *"I'm a forklift driver,"* or *"I'm a businessman."* We aren't the roles we occupy, and we aren't who we were five years ago, for that matter.

Not identifying with a job title can be especially challenging for men because that's how society judges us. We can't blame society for doing this, because that's the history of the world. Our last names came from the name of our jobs. For example, Schmidt was a blacksmith, Miller ran a mill, and Cobbler was a shoemaker. That's what they did, so it was normal for people to say, *"Oh, there's the smith, or there's the shoemaker."*

Men have worked since the beginning of time, and that's how we evolved to describe ourselves. We came from that lineage, but now we're more conscious, and we understand we're more complex. Detaching from your job title can be difficult because it's usually a measure of security. Take the military, for example. Twenty years after a man's left the military, he often clings to his military identity because it's a secure place from which he can operate. He knows who he was there, how to act in that space, and his friends in that sphere understand where he stands.

A lack of power outside of your title or accomplishments always spills over into other areas of your life, including your home life. Many men go home and have absolutely no power. Their wives and kids don't respect them. They often think to themselves, *"I feel like I'm providing. I'm giving money, but my wife nags at me, and my kids willfully disobey."*

"Power" that comes from anything external to yourself doesn't carry over into every sphere of your life. The so-called power you obtain from your identity at work is not actual power. Just like happiness or fulfillment, true power can't be compartmentalized. The universal power we're talking about doesn't come from a title; it comes from within.

Some leaders feel their "title power" should carry into other areas of life. This is due to entitlement and expectation on their part, and because those feelings are associated with their "title power," people are often put off by it. Because of that friction, even the power they feel they should derive from their title is lost.

The external things you do to "be a good husband" don't give you Humble Alpha power. The good things you do that make you a great husband are simply a by-product of who you are. Your true identity will radiate true power and people will feel it. Any title that you do obtain only amplifies the power you already have within. This applies to not only your identity, but your purpose as well.

It's shocking, but in our experience working with some of the most influential people in the world, we've seen that some men pull back into their "title identity" to stay safe because it's their only place of power. We've had public figures and powerful men worth multi-millions of dollars break down on their knees and cry because they don't know who they are. They're not powerful outside of their position, and they feel trapped. What's worse, they can't admit a lack of power because of the expectations of others. They've held onto their title as their identity for so long; what would other people think?

Over the years, Steve Jobs held many positions at Apple—from Vice President of New Product Development to President of the Mac Division to Chairman of the Board of Directors—but in 1983, he stepped away from his role at that time and became the Chief Innovation Officer (CIO) to focus on innovation. He started a division within Apple that competed against the company and even went so far as to move it to a separate building.

Jobs had a pirate flag—a symbol of rebellion—designed and flew it outside their building at Apple headquarters. Needless to say, he drove Apple crazy in the pursuit of better innovation. He put his creative team against the rest of Apple, and, of course, it backfired. Just two years later—in 1985—the CEO fired him.

Jobs, in his early years at Apple, is a perfect example of someone who embodied a role rather than an identity. He thought a change in title or position would change his company's success. It didn't. He tried to navigate the shift by pushing harder. It was the classic do more, work harder—push, push, push model of many leaders. At that time, we bet most people weren't upset that he got fired. The stories of trailblazers who stumbled finding success fill our history books. Some of those stories don't end well, but, thankfully, Jobs' story didn't stop there. He had a meteoric rise and humbling fall. Then, he had an incredible comeback; one of the most spectacular comebacks of all time.

Before his comeback, Jobs started his own company and worked at Pixar; all the while he tried to find himself. He turned Pixar around and made them a multi-billion-dollar company; but that wasn't his passion. Eventually, Apple begged him to return and take over. When Jobs came back to Apple, he went back with more passion and purpose because he knew who he was. Jobs left as someone who, like a chameleon, subtly changed his colors as he changed positions and environments and came back as Steve

Jobs—a man who changed environments and positions because of his colors. He came back as a person who had identified his true self. He had a mission, clarity, and certainty. We all know what happened after that, don't we?

He turned Apple into one of the most influential and valuable companies in the world. It's easily one of the biggest turnarounds in corporate history. Jobs did this by not only realizing who he was but by peeling back the mask and allowing his team to see who he was, too. He started hiring people according to their character, not according to their skill. He wanted people to come up with things that didn't yet exist, and he knew he couldn't train someone to make something that didn't yet exist. He had to cultivate them and give them space to create through the vision, amplified identity, and purpose he concretely communicated to them.

This kind of deep identity work isn't just for someone who's cowering in the corner, not getting anywhere in life. Deep identity work is meaningful and impactful for people who look like they're crushing it. If you want to break out and be the highest version of yourself, you have to get past those outside influences. We call outside influences "stamps on your identity." What stamps are you wearing? You have to move past those external stamps and ask yourself: "How do I show up in this world for real? Who am I as a person? Not as a businessman, mechanic, soldier, special forces guy, or barista.

On this journey, we talk about processes like H.I.T, QOL, and relational capital. We use these methods to help you find your way and navigate through this identity phase of finding yourself. After you internalize these teachings and unleash your Humble Alpha, you'll describe yourself differently. People will notice. They'll see you on the street and look back for a second glance, not because you have big guns but because you have an undeniable presence. They'll remember you, be drawn to you, and love being around you. You'll be different because you'll finally know who you are outside of what you do. Your power will come from within yourself, and it'll be more than most people on the planet have.

Are you ready to get to work? Sit back, grab a pen, and let's get a bird's eye view of how you show up in the world. At the end of this section, we've outlined action steps and questions to take you through finding your identity. Please answer those and, for a deeper dive into finding your identity with even more questions, go to HumbleAlpha-Book.com/Resource and search for "identity." You may make the decision to decide who you are, but what does that look like? Let's discuss what that looks like in the next section.

Becoming a Winner

There is a subtle difference between becoming a winner and chasing wins. You'd think a winner chases wins, but it's actually the opposite. A winner embodies the winner mentality, making the wins simply a byproduct. Let's share an example. Chasing wins means having a single goal, such as: I want to get a nice car, or I want to get a better job. Alternatively, you might have a list of single goals, but they don't tie into a larger picture. Becoming a winner means your success comes from within, and the "wins" in your life emerge from this success. You become the person who has a nice car and travels the globe because it's a byproduct of the lifestyle you live. John Wayne starred in a movie called *The Green Berets,* which familiarized the American public with the real Green Berets. The Green Berets are the Special Forces unit that operates in the U.S. Army. They're highly elite, and it takes two years of significant training to earn the coveted Green Beret.

When I decided to become a Green Beret, I did so because I thought it would be cool to do what they do—blowing stuff up, shooting guns, jumping out of airplanes and helicopters, fast-roping, and other intense activities. I eventually did all of that, and after the training process, I had a big win: I earned the coveted Green Beret. Amid the training, however, I realized a subtle, yet powerful shift in mindset. Instead of merely wanting to obtain the best, I wanted to be the best. I didn't just achieve something great; I stepped into my greatness. Instead of playing for that single win, I became a winner. I adopted the mindset of a winner and became the kind of person who wins as a byproduct of what I carry inside of me.

You might have a goal to create a six or seven-figure business, or to become the CEO of a multi-billion dollar company. If you set those goals, you might achieve them. You might reach that stage, but then what? If you don't possess the kind of lifestyle that sustains those goals and the responsibility that comes with them, what happens? You become more strapped and stressed than before.

Your goal should be to create the lifestyle of someone who owns a seven-figure business or who runs a multi-billion dollar company. You're not setting a goal for a thing; you're setting a goal for an entire lifestyle that's attached to your identity, purpose, and goals so you can turn a complete 360 degrees. Build a vision for the kind of lifestyle that you want to live and the person you want to become, and become a winner, not just someone who wins occasionally.

People with a "business-loser-identity '' chase a title because they think the title will make them feel good. They may also aim for a large revenue goal, because they believe money will afford them things that will make them (or the people they love) happy. A "business-loser-identity" sacrifices family time for business (a real loser move) and tries to be like someone else rather than who they're meant to be. A Humble Alpha focuses on solving problems, elevating others, and amplifying results. The revenue and promotion goals take care of themselves. He is exactly who he is everywhere he goes, and he doesn't become someone different to make an impression. He makes an impression by being himself. A Humble Alpha carves out time to focus on business and time to focus on family, and never places his business or revenue goals above the people he loves.

Having "loser attributes" is all part of the game; we've all had them. When you decide to become a winner, you'll naturally need to let go of the loser. These loser attributes will become the old you, and you'll need a process of letting go of the old you. When it comes to that process, we have you covered.

Letting Go of Your Old Identity

I left for the army in the mid-80s. It was ten days after high school graduation, and I didn't know who the hell I was, but I sported a disco mullet and was cocky as hell. I joined the army because I knew if I stayed home, I'd never get out of the box everyone put me in. In high school, I hated myself. I was terrible at sports. I was the guy who lost every game or match. It didn't matter what sport I played; I lost for the whole team. I left for boot camp full of self-loathing and desperate for change.

When the razor touched my head, and the barber gave me the infamous buzz cut, I thought to myself: *This is the new me; it's who I am now. I'm letting go of that guy whom nobody respected.*

I thought I was a new guy, but one day, we had to complete an obstacle course. It was the kind where you climb a rope, crawl through a tunnel of mud, swing across a river, and make your way through all sorts of difficult challenges. Towards the end of the course, you come to a seven-foot wall that leans toward you at a 15-degree angle. You don't have a rope to help you scale it; it's up to your raw strength and determination. I was the tallest guy in our group, but everyone else got over except for me.

I couldn't get over that wall. The drill sergeant (I'll never forget him) grabbed me by the neck, threw me down in the mud, and put his foot into the back of my neck. He cussed me out like the dirtiest dog you've ever heard until tears filled my eyes, and I jumped up.

I got so mad that in one fell swoop, I flung myself over the wall and landed on the other side. I felt like angels reached down from heaven and gave me a boost. I thought, *Oh my God, that was me the whole time. That was me.* I ran around the wall and did it again. The Drill Sergeant yelled, "Go, go, go." Knowing that I could easily do it twice in a row was the best feeling in the world. From that point on, I knew the only thing that held me back was me. I had an epiphany there. I fully let go of the old me.

I'm not recommending that kind of approach for modern leaders in a corporate environment, but understand the principle of the situation: Most of us have gotten stuck and had the choice to give up or overcome. The difference between giving up or overcoming is the same person, so let go of your former self, but don't forget those past parts of you; use them to empower you.

If you want to become a winner, you can't keep your old baggage and identity. You have to let go of the past to get to the future. When we talk about letting go of your old identity, that doesn't mean you banish it from your life, however. Your past is a part of what you went through to get to this very moment where you're ready to unleash your Humble Alpha, which means it's important to learn from it.

There's a quote that goes, "With no roots, you have no wings." Learn from your roots, but don't let them tie you down. This goes against all of the business gurus who say "burn the ships." They say to get rid of it all and never look back because they're forcing a way forward which is not aligned with their true identity. Force is not the motion or entity we work with. Think about what it looks like to force-feed a child, force someone to do something against his will, or force too many items into a carry-on suitcase you then have to sit on to zip. Frustration abounds. Significant energy is exerted and wasted, and no one feels good about the experience. When force turns into the willingness to do something which turns into the pursuit of and desire for something, then you become a positive force for yourself and all those around you.

We say learn from the past, use it as a reference, and see it as an instructional toolbox or a library. A good friend of ours shares a story of how he's lost and made millions, and even includes that phrase in his bio. People ask him why, if it's old news, he keeps it there, but it's a part of his past that empowers him. He'll tell you that he's learned some of his best lessons from losing millions rather than earning millions. Those losses don't hold him back; they empower him. It's the perfect example of using what you've done in the past to propel you into the future. Everyone says that once you've made and lost your first million, it's easier to make it back because you know how to do it. You don't concentrate on the loss; you focus on how and what you did to earn millions in the first place, and you do it again. Rinse and repeat.

Letting go can be difficult for many people. Some people believe they can't let go or get away from their old identity because they are who they are and their ways are ingrained in them. Even the belief that you can't change or that "this is just the way you are" will set you back. We're here to tell you that your old story isn't set in stone; you have the power to decide to become who you want to be. With that in mind, we have a simple three-step framework for you to use to let go of your old identity.

The first step is to identify what you need to let go of. It may seem obvious, yet so many people don't do this step. They are aware that their lives aren't where they want it to be, yet they carry on thinking and behaving in the same manner. We all have challenges we have to overcome. We go through valleys, experience bad relationships, and struggle to find our way around obstacles. Reflect on your life and identify areas you're not proud of or wish were different. This isn't a place to dwell on, but rather dig into to identify what specifically you need to let go of. If the thought of doing this isn't easy for you, writing them down may help extract the specifics. Journaling and free-writing have significant power to tap into the subconscious mind, which will bring memories or areas that are holding you back to the surface. Once you've identified those areas, it's time to move on to the next step.

The next step is to accept that these setbacks or obstacles have been a part of your life and are a part of your previous story. You can't change the past, so you need to accept the way life unfolded for you. If you don't accept the things you need to let go of, you'll live in a state of guilt and shame. Without acceptance, these behaviors will linger and hold you back. Over and over, you'll be reminded of your old self and experience feelings of guilt and shame each time. Once you've accepted your past, there's one more step.

The final step is to appreciate the old parts of your identity. Acceptance is a fairly neutral act, but appreciation is like giving your old identity a big hug. When you introduce the energy of appreciation, you remove all of the negative feelings about your old identity. You realize that without your old identity, you wouldn't be where you are today. You wouldn't be in the position to grow in the way you can at this moment. When you appreciate all of those things—not just the pleasant ones or significant accomplishments—because you know they're a part of your journey, it's easier to move forward.

When you fully appreciate all that's delivered you to each stage of your journey, you won't be triggered with negative feelings when you're reminded of your old identity. You'll know when you have fully let go of your old identity when you can talk about it without feeling guilt or shame. If you're reminded of your old ways and you feel guilty, then you know you still have some work to do. Everyone has to let go of their old ways, including you. When you grasp these lessons and apply them to your life so that you grow as a person, your roots sprout wings, and you do not only fly the hell out of your dark valley, but you also soar to new heights.

The letting go process is different for each person. Letting go can occur in an instant, or it may need to be worked on over weeks and even months. Don't get frustrated if it takes longer than you think it should. That frustration will only prolong the holding of your old identity. Your old identity may have been your story for decades, give it time.

On my 50th birthday, my wife threw me a party and invited 50 friends. At one point, I stood in front of the crowd, preparing to thank everyone for coming. As I stood there and looked at every single person, I realized I had a story with each of them, and they were all a part of me. I gave a speech that said, "I'm only here, where I am—married to this woman and friends with all of you—because every single one of you played a role in my getting to where I am today." Having my closest friends present was a reminder of being able to hold on to the good and let go of the old me. The humility aspect of the Humble Alpha comes from knowing that you aren't self-made; no one is. Each person plays a role—either showing you who you don't want to become or who you do want to (and can) become.

Claiming Your New Identity

When you let go of your old identity, you have to claim a new one. To claim, according to the dictionary, is to "assert that something is true." Assert that today is the day you become a Humble Alpha.

When defining their new identity, many people don't know where to begin. Use inspiration as a tool to help you clarify who you are. For example, you may have a mentor, teacher, or stack of books that impact you. All of those things are a form of inspiration, and you can use them to point you in the right direction.

When you read or hear something that resonates with you, make a note of it, and dig more deeply. The things that move and inspire you are clues to who you are and what you love. They are threads that help you weave your new identity together. Carry a small notebook and jot your thoughts down or record a message on your smartphone. When I have an epiphany, I immediately send an audio message to my accountability partner, Lane. This makes it real, and I know it won't sit on my phone to one day be deleted without putting it to use. It takes effort and work, but small things like this can have a massive collective impact in your life.

People, mentors, and books are external tools that guide you but don't look at them as anything other than guides. People can lead you in the right direction, but no one can tell you who you are. That's why we open this book with the statement that we won't tell you who you are; you have to figure that out yourself. We do show you tools and proven processes to help you get there. Your job is to take ownership of this discovery process and understand that your new identity is already within; you just have to unleash it.

To help you discover your new identity, we've put together our "identity formula":

IDENTITY = PERSONALITY + HOW YOU TREAT YOUR MIND + HOW YOU TREAT YOUR BODY + HOW YOU TREAT YOUR FAMILY AND FRIENDS + HOW YOU TREAT STRANGERS + HOW YOU TREAT YOUR BUSINESS

The personality part of our equation looks at the "who" and the remaining parts look at the "how." First, let's discuss the personality in detail. We use a two-word moniker because it allows you to specify who you are, yet it's vague enough to leave space for tweaks as you grow. Life is dynamic, and we continually transform. As you step into your higher self, you'll go through regular upgrades. Rather than create a restrictive box, create flexible guideposts.

For example, we've created the Humble Alpha identity. Both attributes describe who we are. Humble reflects our humble approach to always learn from others and elevate. That doesn't mean we think lowly of ourselves; it means we don't feel the need to shout about our power from the rooftops. We're confident, not showy.

The second part—alpha—reflects that we know exactly who we are and we act with purpose in all we do. We dominate in our spheres of influence and rise to the highest levels. We're not hyper-aggressive or controlling (that's where the use of the word humble clarifies the behavior), but we're highly driven and ambitious. This is the personality aspect of the formula; the WHO you are.

The remaining part of the "identity formula" is HOW you interact in the world. How you treat yourself, all those around you, and the entities you're involved in. The reason all of these areas are included is because it allows for the most well-rounded and complete version of yourself to radiate. It's the full integration and balance of life we are going for.

You know those business leaders who treat their businesses as the number one priority, automatically making family and relationships not a priority. You may have been guilty of this in the past. This formula sets the conditions to put emphasis on all areas of life from the start. Moving forward in life, you won't have that imbalance you're probably experiencing right now. You'll see that this full integration will radiate past your identity into everything you do in life, but it begins with your identity.

An example of your identity statement according to the formula up above might be:

> *I am an Avid Innovator who grows my mind daily, keeps my body active and healthy, elevates my friends, supports my family with both my time and resources, always treats strangers with respect, and integrates my life and business fully.*

Wait, where is Humble Alpha? Your personality or two-word moniker will be custom to you. You may define it as a Humble Alpha (that's fine with us), but it has to resonate with you completely. You have complete autonomy to customize your identity as you see fit. When you take full responsibility, you'll actually be stepping into your Humble Alpha, because you are taking control of your identity. Even if your personality may be "avid innovator", you're absolutely a Humble Alpha.

Some more examples of a two-word moniker are Passionate Creative and Generous Visionary. The possibilities are nearly limitless. Whatever you choose, make sure it completely resonates with who you want to become. Don't worry if you're not there yet; that's what this book is about—to help you get there.

This formula covers the absolute basics. We recommend you elaborate as much as you can with as much detail as you can. The better you define this piece, the easier your purpose will jump out at you. Remember, this clarifies WHO you are and HOW you interact in the world. It doesn't tell you WHAT you do. As you define your identity more, be cognizant of the differences.

For instance, "I grow my mind daily" defines how you treat your mind, but it doesn't say WHAT you do to grow your mind. What you do to grow your mind every day may change, but the fact that you DO grow your mind daily doesn't change.

If an identity resonates, it means you talk the talk and walk the walk. We know very powerful people who say they treat everyone with respect, but they treat strangers and servers at restaurants with disrespect and don't care about how their words or actions make them feel. If you say you treat everyone with respect, you better do that, because if this new identity doesn't align, you only fool yourself.

When you define these elements of the formula, write only what truly resonates with you. You may currently treat your body exactly as you want to, "keeping your body active and healthy", so there may be no change to this formula. But how you treat your family and business may need some refinement. Truly look within towards who you want to be and how you want to treat these different areas of your life.

This is the moment where you can decide to be the best version of yourself and step into your Humble Alpha. This formula will help guide you to develop the right habits and routines to step into your best self. You may wonder why we're being so specific in this formula. This is really to set you up to take full ownership of your identity and put focus on it and intentionally live it with all of your being. By having such a clear identity laid out, it makes it that much easier for you to focus on it.

Activating Your Humble Alpha

Once you identify your Humble Alpha identity, it's time to activate it. If you're reading this book, unleashing your Humble Alpha resonates with you, which is why you're here. Remember, you're activating your Humble Alpha as your new identity.

Activate means to "make something operative." How will you operate as this new identity? I like to call the Humble Alpha power the nuclear reactor inside of us. A nuclear reactor is one of the most powerful energy sources on the planet, but you don't see it. It's merely a tiny rod in some water. That's the Humble Alpha inside of us. We don't have to scream and yell about it. Humble Alpha isn't embroidered on our sleeves, written on our name tags, or plastered on our business cards. We don't have to force it. We are who we are because our true identity is deeply rooted in our personality, and it reflects in how we show up.

We shared the example of how everyone knows someone who's a confident leader at work while being shy and unsure of himself at the corporate picnic. He's operating as a title identity, so his true identity isn't active, but buried somewhere under his internal sofa along with the lost change.

If a person says he values work-life balance but spends his entire vacation with his family on his laptop, tablet, or phone, his true identity isn't activated. If his true identity involves balance and Quality of Life and he's not taking charge of his family or rest time, his inner identity is off hibernating with bears in a snowy mountain cave in Montana. It's not activated.

When I'm on vacation with my wife and kids, I focus almost exclusively on them, yet I may schedule an hour every other day (depending on the type of vacation) to do some work. Many vacations, I don't schedule any work time. I can only do this because I'm secure in who I am, and I know that I don't need to drop everything I'm doing to appease someone else or "win a client." Whatever I'm doing, I'm fully present for that moment, and in the rare moments when I am not, my wife feels it and gives me a gentle reminder. I am "humble" enough to heed her reminder.

I talked to a leader recently who takes calls in the middle of the night from clients all over the world. I said, "Just set boundaries for yourself." When you're coming from a place of power and knowledge, then you know how to set boundaries. Trust us. Clients don't think, *"Wow, this person is a jerk"* when you set boundaries. They realize you stand behind your values, which means you're a person of integrity. Who doesn't want to work with a person of integrity?

What's more powerful and sounds more confident—taking calls at 4 a.m. or indicating you're available only from 12 p.m. to 6 p.m.. If people want to talk to you, they find a way. People respect the heck out of that because your expectations of them are clear.

When your identity becomes crystal clear through this process, one of the huge benefits is that you activate that identity in every single sphere you operate in. When you activate, wherever your path veers, you have a quiet belief that you'll crush it. And when you activate your Humble Alpha, it radiates to everyone on your path, whether they're a team member, client, loved one, or stranger. You'll rub off on them, and they'll start feeling like they are able to crush it, too.

Activating your Humble Alpha identity is an intentional drawing a line in the sand to let go of your old identity and step into your new one. Your new identity isn't as much replacing the old, but rather superseding it. This process brings forth your actual identity and allows you to experience true resonance, which you may not have felt in a long time. Activating your identity awakens self-evident confidence, enthusiasm for life, and a feeling of certainty. The value you experience in your life from completing this stage alone more than covers the cost of buying this book. And, we're just getting started.

Before You Continue

As we wrap up this stage (and before you go through the action steps), take a moment and imagine what life will look like when your Humble Alpha identity is crystalized and you're living it fully. What does life look and feel like? How amazing does it feel to interact with the world as your best self? How does it feel to know exactly who you are, because you decided it. Grab your bookmark, save this spot, and put this book down. Do this mental exercise and then continue to the action steps.

Action Steps

Congratulations! You've made it to the end of the first stage. Now it's time to take the knowledge you've acquired and put it into action. We've included action steps below. Some will only take a few minutes, while others may take hours, days, or even weeks to solidify. Don't try to perfect these action steps. Take action and keep making progress. Do the work, take the next action, and let all the action steps in this book build on one another. You've got this.

Remember, action steps are things that are in your control; they are something you can do. They aren't outcomes, which are things outside of your immediate control.

Decide – Decide fully today that there's no turning back. You have decided to become a Humble Alpha, and it's final. You have fully committed yourself to completing all of the action steps in this entire book. In our online resources that come with this book, you can download a contract with yourself to help you remain accountable. Print it out, sign it, and put it where you can see it daily.

1. **Let Go of Your Old Identity** – This is critical for your growth. Along with these steps, we have strategies that allow you to "physically" let go of your old identity. These strategies are complementary, but not necessary. You can find them with our online resources.

a. Identify – List all aspects of your identity that you want to let go of. Write out all you can think of. Be very clear about what they are.

b. Accept – Sit down, think about them, and accept the things you're letting go of.

c. Appreciate – Fully appreciate these aspects for what they are and how they got you to this very moment. Then, let go.

2. **Activate Your Humble Alpha Identity** – Take 1-3 hours to complete this. You may break this step into multiple sessions.

a. Define your 2-word moniker of your personality.

b. Define your HOWs:

i. How you treat yourself

ii. How you treat your mind

iii. How you treat your body

iv. How you treat your family and friends

v. How you treat strangers

vi. How you treat your business

vii. These are the minimum categories. Add as many as you can think of.

c. Begin to live by this identity fully—no turning back!

Be sure to set a deadline for each step. This deadline will ensure you prioritize the action steps and make continual progress. A deadline isn't "I'll have it done 2 weeks from now;" it's looking at the calendar right now, and setting the deadline on the exact date you'll have it complete. Make these action steps a priority in your life.

Bookmark this page to keep track of your next action step. You can also download this checklist, along with other worksheets, resources, and videos that help you dig more deeply into these exercises. These bonuses are free of charge, and they come along with this book. To get them, go to: Humble-AlphaBook.com/bonus

Note: Step 2 in this stage (letting go) will be a continual process for the rest of your life. Put some serious thought to it, take action, and then move on to the next step. As you progress on your journey, use these steps of letting go as needed.

Section Two

UNLEASH

"The purposes of a person's heart are deep waters,
but one who has insight draws them out"

– Proverbs 20:5

One cannot unleash what isn't yet found. Your purpose has always been within you, but you may not have been able to hold it in your hands. Shallow waters are a safe place rooted in security. Deep waters can be rough and unpredictable. Only by exploring the deep waters will you be able to clearly express why you're on this planet.

The insights to draw out your purpose are outlined in this book. Some clues may have been hiding in plain sight, while some have never been brought to the surface. We'll direct a spotlight on the deepest part of you, to help you find your purpose.

Finding Your Purpose

The second stage of becoming a Humble Alpha is all about unleashing. Unleashing means to release from restraint. We help you unleash what's inside of you by first helping you find your purpose. With the understanding that your identity is who you are and how you interact and step into the world, your purpose is what you do. Your purpose drives your vision and mission for your life. As you work through this stage, keep in mind that your purpose always needs to be in alignment with your identity.

For instance, part of your identity may be "I keep my body active and healthy." If you partake in activities that don't make that statement true, then it doesn't fit. Especially if the things you do—such as binge drinking or eating sweets every day—go directly against your identity.

Many people put the idea of finding their purpose on a pedestal. When they do that, they put more pressure on themselves than they need to. Remember, you already have everything you need within, including your purpose. To begin finding your purpose, we have a three-step process.

Step # 1: Known-Knowns

To help you find your purpose, the first step we use is a concept we call "known-knowns." Known-knowns are things you already know or have experienced. Generally speaking, these knowns are what you're good at, stuff you enjoy, and activities where you enter a state of flow. It's essential to look back and reflect on these, because you have to assess what you're starting with.

When my kids start an art project, my wife looks at the supply list. If she doesn't look at that first, everyone gets immersed in the project only to realize they now need glue, and there isn't any. My wife either has to run to the store or stop the project and pick it back up later. Either way, everyone will experience delays and disappointment. You need to know where you're starting, so you know what path to take to get to your destination.

A lot of people have known-knowns they can see, but some can be hazy or even hidden in plain sight. They can't get a clear picture of them, because they've never intentionally focused on this. We have some questions below to help you get clear and dig deeply. Once you write down your known-knowns, you'll experience many revelations and epiphanies. You'll gain significant insight and clarity because now they're on paper.

Some hidden insights can come from those around us. What types of things do friends, colleagues, or family often seek your input about? When my clients look back on these questions, they say things like, "I get asked to do this by my family four times a year" or "Every week, I get asked by a friend to do that." Many clients know what they do well but sometimes are surprised by what they hear. If these talents were previously unknown to you, now they become known.

When you identify your known-knowns, it's just as important to identify the things you don't like to do. These could be areas of business or life, tasks or to-dos, or roles or responsibilities. When you determine what doesn't fulfill you, you can delegate those items to other people or stop doing them altogether. Side note: delegating things you don't like to do isn't "dumping" something on someone; you'll ensure they enjoy doing those activities first. We'll teach you how in the next stage. You'll create a system, business, and lifestyle that minimizes the activities you dislike so you can maximize the things you love (which we help you do throughout this book).

Impact that Resonates

While it's great to do things you like to do, at the end of the day, it needs a component of impact, fulfillment, and meaning. When those aspects are present, you don't face that empty feeling that presents itself in your life with thoughts like, "Well, I made a lot of money, and I helped a lot of people, but it wasn't what resonated with me." Identify the impactful things you've done, but also make sure they fill the vacuum in your spirit. No small act or accomplishment is arbitrary. Don't just stuff your life full of impactful things that don't mean anything to you and go through the motions, all the while you're still empty inside.

Step # 2: Juice in Your Life

The second step we use to help you find your purpose is to identify what adds juice in your life. The juice in life is that which compels you to jump out of bed in the morning. It gets you super pumped about life; it energizes you to the fullest. It's the alignment factor that is the juice. This step is often a little harder because it can be less tangible. Just like before, you can use what inspires you to find the juice in your life.

What are things that you have yet to achieve, but aspire to? You may get inspired by another person's passion, purpose, or accomplishments, look at the root of that inspiration and dig deeply into what it means to you. You're not trying to be that person or replicate his life, but you can emulate what he's doing. A certain amount of emulation is present in everyone's life, but don't compromise on your alignment with your identity in this process.

Another aspect that gives you juice in your life is what you've overcome. Challenges or rough times you've conquered can really give you the juice. This is especially powerful because you don't want other people to go through what you went through. You can, at a minimum, shorten their suffering and help them move on with life faster.

Step # 3: Connecting the Dots

Once you identify your known-knowns and juice, connect the dots. We ask specific questions to help you discover where your purpose shines through without your even knowing. One of the most revealing questions is: What are the activities you enjoy most that people have said made an impact on their life in a positive way? Connecting the dots between the previous two steps allows you to synthesize what is uniquely your purpose.

With my clients, I go through these questions once. Then we sit on them and go through them a couple of weeks later. We go back through them again and again until we uncover core attachments and roots. You can do this on your own or have someone ask you the questions. In my experience, when you have someone else ask you questions, they call you out on your bullshit or shine a light on an area you overlook. As they say, sometimes, you can't see the forest for the trees.

Here are ten questions to help you identify known knowns, juice in your life, and connecting the dots:

Known Knowns

1. What top three things and activities do you enjoy most about your current work?
2. What activities bring you happiness that you want to do more of?
3. What are the types of things you do that friends, colleagues, or family often seek your input for?
4. What's something that, when immersed in it, you lose track of time and get in the flow?

Juice in Your Life

1. If you had all the time in the world to volunteer, what volunteer work would you do that makes you feel great?
2. What significant obstacles have you overcome that you want to ensure no one else has to go through?
3. If you had one year to live, what would you create, and how would you spend your time?

Connecting the Dots

1. What are the activities you enjoy most that people have said made an impact on their life in a positive way?
2. What does your best day look like? What are you doing and just as important, not doing?
3. When only doing the activities that resonate with you at work, how do you enrich your most important relationships?

The first time people answer these questions, they usually do so generically. You have to drill deep. For example, when asked what you like to do, you might reply: I like to fix things. But who do you like to fix things for? You need to drill down on that answer by asking *for whom?* Now, what kind of things do you like to fix? Do you like fixing problems or cars?

Knowing how to drill deeply is a learned skill. Don't worry if it takes some practice. When I work with new clients, they start out answering generically (or vaguely) too. Here's what a typical conversation with a new client might look like:

Me: "What do you do?"

Client: "I help people find clarity."

Me: "What people?"

Client: "Females."

Me: "Clarity in what?"

Client: "Relationships."

Me: "What relationships? Their relationships with their kids or their relationship with their husbands?"

We ask many questions because as you drill down layer by layer, you get to your real purpose. The whole point of this book is to get you to the point where you're doing this kind of deep questioning on your own rather than depending on someone else. The more deeply you dig with questions, the more you uncover passions or attachments to passion. Don't take these questions lightly; they're essential! For even more questions and a deeper dive into this, go to HumbleAlphaBook.com/Resource and search for "epiphany."

When we ask better questions, we get better answers. We're usually better at asking drilling questions of others, but not of ourselves. How many of you have said to someone (maybe your two-year-old or a spouse), stop drilling me with questions?

We don't usually give our own lives the time of day. Most of us don't probe and dig deeply. Seriously—when was the last time you reacted poorly and then said, "Why did you react that way, Joe? What did it trigger? Where did that trigger come from? What do you need to do to release it?"

You can have a list of incredible questions to ask yourself, but if you don't do the work and dig deeply, you're not going to get to the root—to the answers you need to find. You have to go through your answers to these questions four or five times in the beginning until you get to the root. You'll know you're at that root because you'll have a *"That's it!"* moment. Going through the whole process of answering these questions is going to elicit only a fraction of the epiphanies you're going to have if you do the work in this book.

This book is a step forward—a massive step towards finding your identity, figuring out what your purpose is, and discovering where you want to go. It also helps you lay out a strategic plan for getting there. You're putting a puzzle together and peeling back the layers of an onion, which means it can be extensive and exhausting, but you have to do it. It's impossible to move forward if you don't know who you are.

ROSA

To further explore this, we use a trademarked concept known as ROSA. We didn't develop it, but we use it for diving more deeply into who you are. It's a great tool to get unstuck, and many coaches use it.

ROSA stands for reality, objective, solutions, and action.

The reality stage explores what's going on in your life and what you need. It looks at what's happened in your past and what went right or wrong; and how it made you feel. It also looks at how related circumstances made you feel.

The objective stage looks at what your goals are. What do you want in life? What would you like to have? What's your objective in business, life, your relationships, or your career? What's your dream? In a perfect world, how would it be?

The solutions stage looks at how you're going to achieve these goals. How do you get there? We like to ask what you would do at different stages of life to get a unique perspective. If you saw this at four-years-old, what would you do? What would you do if you were a millionaire? Be bold and crazy; think about everything you could do or would do. This exercise is a fun and radical process, and we want you to come up with 40 ideas of potential solutions.

The action stage looks at what you need to do to achieve your objective. What will you do now to put your solution in action? When will you do it? How? Who will help? What else can you do? How long will it take you to do it, and how can you remind yourself to do it? One way to remind yourself to take action is through building routines and stacking habits, which we cover in more detail later in the book.

Macro Purpose

Once you've answered the ten questions above and explored ROSA, you're going to take your answers and come up with a macro and micro purpose. Your macro and micro purpose is a framework that adds clarity to your life and helps you unleash your Humble Alpha. We don't ask questions to ask questions. You answer the questions and do something with your responses.

When we look at life, there's a macro picture and a micro picture. The macro is a big picture. It's your entire life summed up in one or two simple sentences. It's similar to the constitution because we base it on principles. We keep it very thematic and somewhat vague because it needs to be flexible. What resonates with you at 20 years old might not at 60 years old, but you should see the common thread. If you look back at any one's life, you'll be able to follow the common thread.

Some examples of a macro life purpose are:

- Create art that makes people happy
- Connect great people to make amazing things for people
- Elevate others, leaving them in a better place than you found them
- "To create an exciting future and colonize Mars."—Elon Musk

Your macro purpose is your life's calling, and it will guide you for the next 30 years or more. By coming up with a clear macro purpose, you'll have more clarity as you move forward. What makes this even more compelling is that it's a universal statement anyone can get behind.

Take, for example, my macro purpose of elevating others. I've done that since I was a kid. It's what I learned from my grandfather, and it's a constant in my life. Whether I'm working as a consultant or on an oil rig doing underwater welding, it's still my purpose and a thread you'll see throughout my life. Your macro purpose aligns with how you treat everyone around you and how you invest in relational capital. What I do to elevate others may change, for example, as I gain more influence, but I'm always elevating.

Take a look at Elon Musk. His macro purpose for life is very apparent. He mentions it often, and if you've read his biography, it's literally two words: Colonize Mars. What he does will change as he progresses, but the overarching theme will stay the same.

Your macro purpose is a true purpose, not a job. It's not something you do to make money. You'll find your macro purpose in your heart, but you have to dig deeply to find it. It's critical that you are 100% honest at this point and don't try to fool yourself. Putting something down because you think it's the right answer will not work. Writing something down because you think you should, will not work.

When you're crystal clear about your identity and you've thought deeply on the 10 questions we shared earlier, your macro purpose is easier to define.

Micro Purpose

Your micro purpose is what you're living right now. If your life were a book, your micro purpose is the chapter you're living right now. To define it, we ask questions such as: What are the things I need to do in this chapter in life? And are those things aligned with my macro purpose? Write down the activities or accomplishments you need to work towards now. As you do that, you may identify something you want to do, but not right now. That's perfectly fine; put it on the back burner as a written goal for the future.

Write down your micro purpose with the understanding that this life chapter sets up the next life chapter, and you're always building upon it. Your next chapter in life will be easier if you do this.

If you look at Elon Musk, he's building Space X—the vehicle to get to Mars. He runs Tesla, with its solar-powered vehicles. He's also the Chairman of SolarCity—a company with a complementary mission to store energy for the residential sector. He's doing everything he needs to do in this life chapter to see his higher macro purpose realized. Elon Musk is a perfect example because some of his businesses are just for fun, which is part of life too. They still play a role in that vision of colonizing Mars because they keep his life exciting.

Elon Musk is an extreme example of a billionaire doing amazing things. You're going to do amazing things, too, so look at the principles we're talking about here. You can apply these same principles and identify what you need to do in this life chapter to become a Humble Alpha. Everything you accomplish in this chapter sets you up to be successful in the next and, ultimately, with your life's purpose. Everything that you do—every project, every business that you start or invest in—affirms your life purpose.

Once you've answered the questions, probed deeply, and defined your macro and micro purpose, you're ready for the next stage—the Epiphany stage—where you test and validate.

Epiphany

After going through the exercises mentioned in the past chapter, you'll have many answers that may have taken days or weeks to formulate. It's important not to focus on getting your Macro and Micro Purpose "perfect," because the next step is to test and tweak, if necessary. In this step, you will test and validate your Macro and Micro Purpose to see if they resonate. You might find that something you wrote down doesn't. For example, the idea of being an entrepreneur might entice a lot of people, but when they take that leap, they may not like it. You'll only know from experience. By testing and validating these ideas, you get to that all-important certainty. That's the epiphany.

Let's break down the concept of an epiphany. When was the last time you had an epiphany, and what happened? How did it happen? How did it start? Did it come out of thin air, or did something happen that caused it? An epiphany can come unexpectedly, but you can set the conditions to where an epiphany becomes a given byproduct.

The best way we've found is to go out and take action. Do the things you wrote down as part of your identity. Do things that are part of your purpose. You need unrelenting intention toward this effort. When you experience all of the things you wrote down, we guarantee you'll gain many insights. We want to be clear, this doesn't mean you need to hustle 24/7. Validating your identity and purpose doesn't require grinding, but it does require an unquenchable thirst to see it through.

If you said you wanted to treat strangers with respect, go do it. If you said you want to build something incredible, start with the first step. Everything you do will be with the utmost intention. You will quickly realize if these things are what you really want. You'll begin to feel a sense of energy that you may have not felt before. You may feel an enthusiasm you haven't felt since you were a kid. This feeling of resonance and epiphany is what you are looking for, and you'll find it, if you follow this process. The process is simple, yet it's profound if you do the work.

While you're doing the external work to gain certainty, we've also found that doing some internal work by asking questions helps greatly. Ask yourself:

1. What's not working right now?
2. What have I tried to make it work?
3. Why do I think it didn't work?
4. What can I do now?

When you go through the questions, you might list out things like "I tried to grow my business, and I scaled;" "I've hired a coach;" "I hired a funnel team," etc. List out everything you did that didn't work, then ask yourself: What am I missing? Why didn't it work? What do I think it was? As you do that, you might come up with your answer right away and say, "It's because I was outsourcing. I wasn't doing the work. I was expecting someone else to do my job for me. I wouldn't expect someone else to make me successful instead of doing it myself."

Many people fail at a task because they don't give themselves permission to stand up and do it themselves. They think things like: *I'm going to hire this guy, and he's going to do this, and I'm going to do that.* Then suddenly, they're sitting in the same position years later, having made no forward progress. I know a guy who spent $250,000 on his online sales funnel and sold less than $9,000 worth of product. That's because he just wanted someone else to do it for him. When you have that mentality, you run into situations where people take your money and run. Not necessarily on purpose or maliciously, but it happens because they're not you, and they don't have your vision, mission, or passion. They can't. No one will ever replace you. No one can do what you do. Even if they do the same thing, you do it differently.

All of a sudden, you realize you waited for someone else to make you successful. There's your epiphany. Once you come to that understanding, you can take responsibility for what happened. You can only step into your greatness when you take responsibility for why you are where you are. From there, it's onward and upward.

When testing, your intention and attention is vital to realizing insights and epiphanies. This boils down to focus, which comes in a few forms. You'll want to know how to best use focus to your advantage so you can minimize the time it takes to validate your purpose.

Directing Your Focus

There's an adage that says, "What you focus on is what you get." When most people talk about focus, they talk about laser focus. They tell you to direct your full attention towards something and put blinders on so you don't see anything else. We don't do that. When we talk about focus, we talk about one of the most powerful aspects of success, and that's the ability to have a wide vision *while focusing*.

Why? Well, if you ask any successful person, you'll find that about 30% of their success comes down to two factors: luck and coincidence. If you're hyper-focused on one thing only, you don't see what's on the left and right of you, which is where success hangs out when you look at coincidence and luck.

That's why we talk about the macro and micro. You need to see the big picture, even when you're focusing. That focus is vital, but remember, you're focusing on the picture of the lifestyle you want, not just the things you want to get.

If you're Elon Musk, your first step is not to focus on saving enough money to buy a rocket ship to go to Mars. Your first step is to create a battery-powered car, so you have something to drive on Mars and to explore alternative energy sources. Do you see the difference? The rocket ship will come when you build the lifestyle that leads to that rocket ship. You focus on the lifestyle—the macro— while you're doing the day-to-day elements.

Your micro or daily activities must always align with your macro. Unless you keep the macro in mind, you won't know whether what you're doing is aligned or not. Without the big picture in mind, you'll veer off on a completely different path, only to realize you've traveled in the wrong direction the whole time.

Earlier in the book, we discussed the difference between going for a win and becoming a winner. This concept plays a role in directing your focus. To give you a straightforward example, we see people on the internet all the time who say they want to buy a Bentley. Let's say they save $250,000 and go out and buy a Bentley. Then they realize they need insurance, a garage, a security system, and an $8,000 oil change every quarter. They forgot they wanted the lifestyle of someone who can afford to drive a Bentley.

Focus and Flow

Focus creates your reality. Knowing what not to focus on is just as important as knowing what to focus on. When you can differentiate between what to focus on and what not to, you can get into a flow state. Focus and productivity are two different things. For example, focus enables you to get two hours of work done in 40 minutes. Productivity would be allocating those 40 minutes to a time during the day when you're most on fire.

We won't go into too much detail on flow, because it's a vast topic, but flow allows us to tap into periphery opportunities while keeping the big picture in check. When we're in the flow, we don't have tunnel vision or put blinders on. It allows us to see almost everything, and we let go of the small details that keep us stuck. We're moving and grooving, and we know what we need will come to us, whether it's an epiphany, the right person, or a proper connection. We can stay in flow with what we're doing because we know that when we need the next thing to keep moving forward, it'll raise its hand. We'll see it flagging us down because our eyes are open while we're focused.

The more you practice getting into flow and focusing, the more you'll get comfortable knowing that the next step will present itself at the right time. Intuition is a crucial piece for directing your focus and getting into flow, which we'll talk more about later. We also have apps, a wearable device, and strategies that help people get into the flow state almost instantly.

Your Focus Cave

We like to use what we call a focus cave to direct our focus. A focus cave is a physical place that acts as a sanctuary to dive deeply. Cal Newport wrote an excellent book centered around this topic called Deep Work that talks about this in length. The idea of a focus cave is that you're setting your conditions and surroundings in the most advantageous way so you can focus.

This focus cave sets up the conditions for you to do your best work. By surrounding yourself with the most advantageous triggers, conditions, and environment, you can more easily direct your focus. The focus cave is a concrete example of what you can (and should) do for the rest of your life anytime you need to dive deeply.

In addition to my focus cave, I use proprietary wearables that I put in my ears along with a few other things we introduce in our Humble Alpha Leadership Program. I can sit down for two hours and polish off a whole day's worth of work. In your focus cave, you're incredibly focused but also incredibly aware. In a cave, sounds echo. You hear things in your focus cave without operating in a tunnel.

When you go into your focus cave, however, you have to employ discipline. Eliminate all distractions. Shut everything off; leave everything on the outside. Turn your phone, Facebook, Twitter, Instagram, and all other media off. If you want to go deep and create an incredible life—one where you can do what you want when you want with whom you want wherever you want—it depends on you. No one's going to do it for you. In the big scheme of things, it's a simple thing to turn off your damn phone. Put it aside for two hours, focus on your work, and kill it. If you can't do that, reread this book. Go back to the beginning.

Creating Strategic Deadlines

Another component of directing your focus is creating strategic deadlines. When we create a strategic deadline, we set a specific due date, such as December 1st. For instance, you can put a deadline on defining your macro and micro purpose a week from today. But you need to put the exact date, not "a week from today." Sometimes, we don't hit that deadline because we didn't prioritize our goal or project. We might push it back because we think we have next year, next summer, or next quarter. When you don't create a deadline for a goal or project, it easily gets kicked down the road. My clients often say they'll try to do what I ask them to do. I look at them and ask, "Try? Give me the day and time when you'll have it done." You either want to do something, or you don't.

We're very fortunate to be alive today because we have so many opportunities. Because we have so many opportunities, however, we're spoiled. We sit around waiting for things to happen to us—if they happen at all. If they don't, we often complain about it. You can't sit around and wait for things to happen. You have to take charge of your life. This may sound like old news, but most put deadlines for work-related stuff, yet not on the most important things in their personal development. Decide to take this journey toward becoming a Humble Alpha seriously and make deadlines.

Blocks of Focus Time and Focus Music

You can use any avenue to focus and anything to your advantage to set up the right conditions. Strap on your earphones, listen to Brain.fm, and employ other techniques you find helpful. If you get distracted, identify what's causing it and minimize those distractions. You have to identify and eliminate distractions and determine what focus advantages to set up so you can crush it.

There are many tools to help build your focus. Sleep is one of them that's easy to overlook but easy to implement. Meditation is also a tool that energizes you to focus on your goals. In this book, we expose you to many different concepts, ideas, and strategies to help you live your best life. We can't go into detail about every concept, but we can expose you to them. Meditation may resonate with you. Getting better sleep may be your ticket, or you may want to design your focus cave. Employ all of these strategies or one. What you need to decide is to look into the thread that calls out to you and determine to do more research or learn more about our Humble Alpha Leadership Program by visiting: https://humblealphabook.com/bonus

Focus is about being intentional with what's most important. When it's time to work, your work is most important. Your work ties your life chapter, life purpose, and identity together. If it takes a lot of effort to focus or you have to try hard, you're probably not having fun doing what you're doing, and you're likely not going after your life's purpose. If you'd rather hang out on Facebook instead, then what you're doing isn't your purpose. Start over and figure out why you're here on this planet.

When we talk about focus, this isn't something we made up. It's not a theory. We live our lives this way. Between the two of us, we've traveled the world and lived abroad in places like Panama and countries throughout Europe because we've wanted to and focused on those goals. One of my life's missions was to travel to Europe and live in different countries. I want to reiterate that because a lot of people write books based on a learned theory. We don't just base our practices on studies or methods; we've implemented these ideas in our lives over the last 20 years and have seen tremendous success. Our clients have too. What we teach you is real; there's no question we can't answer about these processes because we literally own them.

As a Humble Alpha, you choose to cut out every distraction (even if it's chasing women) and focus on what you need to do because it powers you even more toward your purpose. It allows you to amplify your Humble Alpha around the world. Honing your focus will do wonders in your life. When you stack it with the right habits and routines, you have a powerful combination.

Building the Habits and Routines

I worked for a large company with around 90 locations across nine countries in Europe. The CEO would be in the middle of something and say, *"Okay, I have to go meditate. See you in half an hour."* He'd always do it with respect but walk out no matter where he was. He earned more respect than prominent, loud leaders declaring they were kings. We were all amazed at his discipline, and knew him as a person who cares, knows what he's about, and is uncompromising with his values. His habits and routines helped build his reputation and inspired others.

Having the right habits and routines is a crucial component of unleashing your Humble Alpha. We use a lot of techniques discussed by James Clear in his book *Atomic Habits*. Habit stacking is one of those techniques because it's very straightforward, and it works.

If you set a goal, how do you start going in that direction? What habits do you need to create to get there? And, how do you create a habit anyway? Repetition is the mother of all learning. If you want to create a habit to meditate in the morning and wake up tomorrow and say, *"Damn, I forgot. I'll do it tomorrow."* Well, tomorrow never comes. How do you fix that? Through habit stacking.

Habit stacking works like this: If I get up every morning and the first thing I do is grab a cup of coffee, then I put my journal or earphones for my meditation app next to the coffee pot. If I want to journal what I'm grateful for before bed every night, when I make my bed in the morning (which is the first step to a successful day!), I put my journal on my pillow so when I go to bed, it's there. That's called habit stacking. You stack habits one on top of the other, so you don't forget, and that creates a new habit.

As you stack all of these habits on top of each other, you're moving towards your goal. What's magical about this process is that it creates certainty that you will get to where you want to go. You don't have to worry about how you're going to get there anymore because you have the habits and procedures in place to drive you down that road on autopilot.

When I first started habit stacking, I had reminders in my phone five times a day. I quickly realized that was too much, so I knocked it down to only two times a day. Some people have reminders but still skip them. When they're in the middle of something, the reminder will go off, and then they don't do it so they can finish up what they're working on. If you say you'll do it later, you won't. Prioritize the most important meetings you have every single day. Every habit you do is a meeting you have with yourself. I don't care who you are; you have to meet with yourself. If you aren't meeting with yourself every day, you're not the CEO of your life enterprise. You have to take care of yourself. You have to answer to all the stakeholders, and who is a stakeholder in your life? You are!

When you start stacking habits, setting reminders, and stopping what you're doing to implement them immediately, you'll grow in ways you cannot imagine. With my gratitude practice, if I'm on the phone and my alarm goes off, I respectfully tell that person. I add him or her to my list of who I'm grateful for, and I say to that person something along the lines of, *"I'm grateful for you; thanks for letting me interrupt you with this."*

If you have bad habits you want to change, the good news is changing them is easier than creating new ones out of thin air because you already have a reminder. In his book *Atomic Habits*, James Clear talks about the three Rs. The first R stands for reminder; this is a notification that acts as a trigger to do something. The second R stands for routine, and the third R stands for reward.

To replace an old habit, you take the second R—the routine—and replace it with the new thing that you want to do. That means the first thing you need to do is identify the bad habit you want to replace. Make a list of the bad habits and the habits you want to replace them with. We talk about this in-depth in our goal-setting course available at qolenterprises.com, but the most important thing to note is that your new habit must be more advantageous and aligned with your new identity and purpose. By replacing an old habit with something new and upgraded, enthusiasm enters your life because you know what you're doing is better than what you used to do. We all have bad habits, and we'll continue to pick one up that we need to replace with a better, more improved one. That's life and growth.

Even with habit stacking, it can be difficult to change, especially with bad habits you've had for decades. To make it easier, set the bar very low with the new replacement habit. For example, when it comes to working out, the first step in your new habit might just be putting on your running shoes. Many people who go all-in immediately don't always make it.

The people who set the bar incredibly high or hold an impossible standard often make the new habit too daunting. The new habit becomes this huge mountain, and they look at it and think, *How am I going to climb this?* Instead, if you focus on how to get up the little ridge that's 20 feet away, it becomes much easier. You can do that.

Using the example of working out: If you want to do push-ups, instead of saying I want to do 50 push-ups, start with 5. Then you set up a reminder or a trigger, whether that's a note on the bathroom sink or an alarm on your phone. Now, when you set the bar low and do 5 push-ups, you begin to realize that's too easy. When you start to do the activity, what you'll find is that after you do 5, you say to yourself: *Well, I'm already here. I guess I can do 25.* As you continue to build that habit, your confidence will increase and it'll be easier and easier to maintain the habit.

The world of instant gratification and overnight success causes a lot of people to fail. Reality TV highlights amateurs who've never sung before and got a contract overnight. People expect that now, and it creates unrealistic expectations of oneself. The most successful people learn to enjoy the process of progress. You can't build Rome in a day, right? While we say this, we know there are always exceptions to the rule, but they're rare.

Don't pressure yourself to reach goals that are way out of your league at this moment. If I said I want to do 2,000 push-ups every day, I know right now I would never do 2,000 push-ups every day—ever. On top of that, it's 99% likely that 2,000 pushups in a day is arbitrary, not linked to my identity and purpose. Start with where you can start and move forward. You're building a foundation to create something that's going to be real and sustainable in your life.

Why do you think so many people fail at diets? Why do you think so many people set goals and don't reach them? Because the goals they set are ridiculous. If you want to stop drinking, stop smoking, pay all of your bills early, never eat ice cream again, quit your job, and start a company all on January 1st, that's unrealistic. It's not going to work. When you set those goals, your subconscious and intuition know they're not going to happen all at once, if at all.

We've talked about the reminder and routine components of the three Rs, let's talk about the reward. A lot of people like to eat a piece of chocolate when they do something they're supposed to do, or they allow themselves to buy something. The reward you choose has to be in alignment with the life you have and the life you want to live. If you're big into wellness, doing a wheatgrass shot rather than eating a piece of chocolate would be a reward in alignment with who you are and what your ultimate goals are.

Set a reward so when you do what you said you would (or don't do what you said you wouldn't), you have an incentive. Now, some people actually work better with punishment than rewards. For example, if they have to pay $500 bucks if they do something they said they wouldn't, it becomes an excellent accountability tool. As a Humble Alpha, you know yourself well and know which option is best for you.

Habits become routine through repetition and momentum. You'll shift your habits and tweak them as you practice. For example, if you want to build a habit to meditate for 10 minutes and after a while, you feel like you can go a little longer, you might start meditating for 15 minutes. You'll shift and move the goal post because building habits and routines is an ongoing process that extends throughout your life.

Airplanes have auto-pilot and so do we. The majority of our behaviors are on auto-pilot or default settings. Every experience and thought you've had helps shape the default behaviors that are running your life right now. You, your body, and your mind are a living memory medium; every present moment, you imprint information into your memory. Your current habits and routines confirm your existing default. When you create new habits and set reminders you stick with, you eventually create a new default for yourself.

Your new default is the Humble Alpha. After a while, your new habits take less thought and attention because auto-pilot begins to take over. You won't even think about them. It's like driving a car; you don't have to think about it anymore, but when you first got your license, you did.

When you solidify a new habit and routine and then, for some reason, miss it, you'll jump back into it. For example, if you get into a routine of working out and going to the gym every morning and then get sick, you can't wait to jump back in. You almost have withdrawal symptoms because you miss your new habit and routine. With the gym, hormones and social components give it a bigger kick than other habits; some habits are like that. When you work out, your body releases endorphins—the happy hormones. You meet people and talk to them every day, and discover like-minded friends. Therefore, if you miss the habit, you quickly recognize something is missing from your life, so it's easy and natural to jump right back in.

Getting clear on your purpose, becoming ultra focused, and crystalizing your habits and routines help you grow in many tangible and intangible ways. You'll realize incredible growth in the exact direction you desire. Eventually, you'll hit a growth plateau. It's almost always caused by an unforeseen area: a blindspot.

Identifying Blind Spots

Blind spots are things we can't see. It doesn't matter who you are; you have blind spots in some areas of your life. You can have your life all figured out, be on top of your game, super in-tune, and aware, but there will always be a blind spot you need to deal with and overcome. If you don't become aware of that, it's going to hold you back. You can grow, progress, and achieve, but eventually, you'll hit a plateau. That plateau is almost always rooted in a blind spot. You don't know what you don't know, so by merely knowing that you have blind spots, you're a step ahead.

When it comes to blind spots, you almost always need someone else to help you identify them. The person you permit to point out your blind spots must be on a similar path to yours and be more experienced or specialized in that particular area. A lot of people make the mistake of getting well-intentioned, but unqualified people to help them identify blind spots. As a coach of 20-some years, I've seen how dangerous it is for people to get advice from well-meaning but unqualified individuals.

Who you ask to help you has a lot to do with your purpose and identity. If you feel you need to let go of anger, your first instinct may be to ask people within your circle. The problem with that is all those within your current circle likely have the same anger issues you do. So it would be better to find someone who's overcome that issue completely. It doesn't matter the subject—whether it's letting go of anger, business success, or blind spots you may have—the key is to find someone qualified who is ahead of you. Accessing the highest level available to you is a best practice, because it shortens the learning curve. I always say this: "If you want to get somewhere, find someone who's there and ask them how they did it." It's that simple. I've never had anyone who I've asked to be my mentor tell me no. I've approached 85-year-old men who are out-of-this-world successful, and I've made them feel honored by asking. People love sharing their knowledge and wisdom.

Anyone who has knowledge and success will always share it, but if you're looking for quick solutions for your problems, you aren't looking for a mentor, you're looking for a coach. A mentor holds a mirror up and says, "What do you see? Have you thought about this?" If you look through time, you'll see a chain of mentors linked together; everyone's connected somehow.

As you move forward and continue to validate your purpose, finding a mentor is a great way to help you identify your blind spots. After experimenting and validating, you'll still likely have things you need to work out. If you need a course correction, a mentor can quickly guide you in the right direction

When a person who is 50, 40, or 30 years older than you, with a great deal of experience, sits across from you, he'll ask one question and reveal your blind spot. Suddenly, you'll see it. You don't know what you don't know. If you aren't humble enough to take it and run with it—to experience it and embrace it—then you're not there yet. These people are there. I mentor about six people right now, and I'm hardcore. I tell them how it is. I help them collapse time, see their blind spots, and move forward more quickly. Collapsing time is essentially taking something that would typically take a long time, and shortcuting the solutions from someone who has that experience and can lead you through the minefield. You have a blind spot — big deal. You didn't know; now you do, no one knows everything.

When you look at your blind spots, be humble enough to accept them. No one likes to work with, partner with, or coach individuals who act like they're perfect and know everything—including us, which is why we don't accept them into our programs. If a person says he knows everything, we advise him to come back when he realizes he's not perfect. We're the first to tell you we are not perfect. Any individual who works with us has to believe that together we can be much better than we are as a single unit.

Identifying a blind spot can have an immediate impact on your revenue. I once had a client who owned a roofing company. He was stuck; he couldn't get past $100K per month no matter what he tried. I came from the consulting world and ran a bunch of my own companies, so he scheduled a video call with me. He went over his business, revenue, and costs. The first thing I asked was: *"Do you have warranties for the roofs you put on?"*

He replied, *"Everyone has a warranty."* The rest of the conversation went like this:

Me: *"But, do you have a warranty?"*

Client: *"Well, yeah, I have the factory warranty."*

Me: *"How much would it cost to double that warranty and the worker warranty for ten years?" Ask the insurance company."*

It was $100 bucks for a policy— one hundred dollars. We raised my client's prices to cover the warranty and increased his profit due to the value of the 10-year warranty. We tacked on about $500-$800 per roof, and that brought him well above $100,000 per month. We cracked the revenue ceiling within the first 30 minutes of the very first call. If you can imagine, this is how you crack a blind spot, and it happens every single time we talk to someone.

In another part of our business, we have what's called Immediate Impact Revenue where we outline three ways to grow a company. As most people know, those three ways are: more clients, higher prices, and repeat sales. Underneath those three categories are 35 proven strategies to do these exact three things. Whatever you're not doing, we help you do, and it immediately boosts your revenue. That's one example of the revenue impact of identifying a blind spot.

If you could see everything, you wouldn't need help. You wouldn't be stuck. We need to identify blindspots and overcome them continually. When you identify your blind spots, you face the storm inside of you and calm it. That's what you do as a Humble Alpha. You won't get a reward for doing it or a badge to wear that says, "I check my blind spots." It's going to be who you are. When you get into the habit of identifying your blind spots, you get into a position to amplify your purpose.

Amplifying Your Purpose

Amplifying your purpose involves tapping into what's already within you, using the resources you have, and asking the right people for help. You must be crystal clear on your identity and individual purpose. When you're crystal clear and seeking assistance, other people can determine how they fit into the bigger picture. You can amplify your purpose with partnerships, joint ventures, businesses that you start, or by investing in projects. There are many ways to amplify your purpose, and you want to do so because this is where real impact and fulfillment can happen.

One way that we amplify our purpose is through something we like to call radiant value. Radiant value is the value you create that passes through the person you created it for and into another person. It's a chain reaction. It moves from person to person to person; that's radiant value! When you possess much-needed knowledge and collaborate with a company, you help that company owner learn to do what you do. He then helps his executives and so forth.

For example, I have a speechwriter named Neil Gordon. Through writing for me, he read my speech about radiant value. A couple of weeks later, he called me to tell me the concept of radiant value changed his life. One day, he was on a walk with a client who had a client (say that three times quickly!) who wanted his client to introduce her to another coach his client knew. She feared to make the introduction because she didn't want her client to leave her and hire the other coach.

All he suggested is for her to think about the radiant value she would create by giving her client full permission to have her own experience with that other coach. He said, *"Consider the radiant value you give to the world by doing that.*" The concept blew his client away. She made the introduction, and her client is even more committed to her than ever before because she didn't have a scarcity mindset. She created value for her client that's being transferred to the rest of the world. In other words, she amplified her purpose.

On a much larger scale, another example of this involves the time I met Olivia Newton-John on a beach in Jupiter, Florida. After Desert Storm and the Iraq War, the military gave me anthrax vaccinations and other injections, and I was exposed to sarin and cyclosarin nerve gas. When I got out, I was on a journey to cleanse my liver, kidneys, and system from all of those things. The doctor told me I couldn't; that it was in there forever.

It was through a friend that I met Olivia Newton-John on the beach that day. She and her husband, Amazon John Easterling, had a company at the time called Amazon Herb Company. They grew and sustainably harvested herbs from the Amazon Jungle through (and with) the Shipibo Indians. They also gave 10% of the revenue back to the Shipibo Indians, so they could buy their land, which they should have already owned. The Shipibo Indians are the only tribe in the entire Amazon Rainforest that owned their land due to Olivia and her husband's company.

That's an excellent example of radiant value right there. Another example of radiant value is that they didn't fumigate the herbs brought in from the Amazon. They let them sit at the border for 45 days to bypass the fumigation process and then brought them into America. I started using them, and the results were incredible. I started healing.

The third example of radiant value is that I was so crazy in love with this product that I helped launch John and Olivia's company in six countries in Europe. We made a thriving business out of it and made a lot of money. That radiant value exploded across Europe. There's a long story behind why it didn't continue: the European Union and the pharmaceutical industry shut it down; the herbs were too potent because they were a direct source liquid extract and not pills, etc. They blocked us, but in the end, we touched probably 100,000 people with this one idea of sustainably harvesting a plant in the Amazon and giving back to a tribe so they could own land that should've been theirs. The entire world got involved. That's incredible radiant value.

When we presented the questions that help you find your purpose, we mentioned how challenges you've overcome can potentially fuel your purpose. Battling those toxins for years really took its toll, but when I found something that helped me overcome them, I knew in my heart I needed to help spread it as far as I could. I knew that at least for a short time, helping others remove toxins and poisons from their body was my purpose. By aligning efforts with John and Olivia, I was amplifying my purpose on a large scale. How powerful is that? Remember this particular story, because we'll discuss it from another perspective later in the book.

Life Enterprise

The final step in this stage is what we call life enterprise. Your life enterprise is just like a business enterprise. You are the CEO of your life enterprise. Who does the CEO answer to in a business enterprise? He or she responds to the Board of Directors and stakeholders. Well, you could argue that your Board of Directors is your family, and the stakeholders are anyone else in your life.

A CEO in a business enterprise has to make sure that the stakeholders are happy. The same goes for your life enterprise; you make your stakeholders happy by elevating them. Leave every single person you run into every single day in a better place than when you met him or her. Do this with everyone from the postal worker to the bag lady to your neighbor, wife, kids, family, and friends. Ask yourself: How is it that I can leave this person in a better place than when we started talking? When you do this over and over again, it becomes a habit. Take for instance a random stranger I elevated many years ago.

When I lived in Berlin, I took visitors on a river cruise to see the city from another vantage point. While on the ship with two friends, I spotted a man sitting by himself, sweating something awful while reading a newspaper.

He was sitting alone, just behind us. The sun was beating down on us, so I went to get drinks for my friends and asked him if he wanted something. Surprised, he looked around and said, "Yes." Upon my return, I invited him to join us, which he did.

We ended up becoming the best of friends; he also happened to be a member of the Swedish/German royal family. We met almost every day to discuss life and society, and he took me down a new path of understanding and articulation. The German language is especially good for being precise and he showed me the art of masterful communication.

I met his girlfriend and we became a tight-knit group of friends. Some time after, I met their extended family (who are also members of the same royal family). I was privy to meeting those who walk the halls of history. Later, I took part in founding their political pressure group which turned into a party and now has seats in just about every German State. I have learned more from my friend, Sven, than any other single person in my life, and he has raised my societal impact consciousness as well as my profile among the German elite and political establishment.

My opinion is listened to and respected when it comes to EU and US policy, trends, and thoughts about what may or may not be. I have been on German TV many times, and it has made me a trusted personality.

All of this happened because I took the time to elevate a random person on a ship cruise. Now, 15 years later, we're inseparable, and I have a whole new arena in which I operate. What did that cost me? A beer and a minute.

When I'm recording a video and my family accidentally comes in, I momentarily stop what I'm doing. I'm responsible for them. I see myself as their provider. My wife has her own company, but still, in my mind, I'm a provider. It's part of who I am. It's part of my identity. I provide for myself, my family, and for the world around me. In your life enterprise, you should strive to apply and live out every principle we discuss.

I have clients come to my home in Hungary to do coaching by osmosis for a week. They observe and interact with my family and me. They see that when the family arrives, we take a break. They understand how important it is at dinner time that we sit down with each other and have a face-to-face connection. Living out your values is part of being a Humble Alpha. You take charge of your life, but you're not selfish either. By understanding who you are and what your purpose is, it's easy to elevate others everywhere you go. It's actually a byproduct. You do what you want, and yet everyone around you is happy. How does that happen? By going on this journey.

Relational capital is another critical component in your life enterprise. If you invest in those around you by elevating them, the next level is to invest in a relationship with them. How do you build relationships? The first step is to take a look at the stakeholders in your life. You may or may not know them, but become interested in their lives and give them genuine compliments about something you notice or that touches you. Make real and genuine connections. Make people feel good not to check the box, but because you truly care, and you must truly care for it to come across as genuine. When you're aware of the roles people play in your life and how other people have elevated you to get you where you are, it's super easy to do that.

After investing in relational capital, find ways to work together or collaborate. Doing so creates massive opportunities. It creates influence you can wield to make a lot of money and have a lot of impact. You'll always get a return on the investments you make in relational capital. I like to say it is the safest investment in the world.

What we've talked about thus far in this book has been about you as an individual: your identity and your macro and micro life purpose. All of this has to do with your thoughts, behaviors, and how you interact with the world. You have to figure this out to be a positive influence in the world. Of course, you can do great things in the world, but when you get crystal clear on who you are and what you're supposed to do, the results are massively more influential.

The impact you can have on people's lives is far more significant because you know who you are. You don't need other people or things to fill your cup. It's already full and overflowing. You have an abundance mindset. You're wealthy not just with your finances, but with your family, relationships and with an endless source of drive from within. From that knowing and secure place, you can provide everything you need to provide for yourself, other people, and your life enterprise. When I give, I give because I want to, not because someone has placed a burden of expectation on me.

As we wrap up this stage on purpose, it's important to note that the first two stages are all about you as an individual. As we move forward in the book, we'll be discussing things outside of yourself, such as your organization and everything outside of that. Your identity and purpose will have an enormous effect on the company you have, and what you do inside your company. Ensure as you move forward in life, that your individual identity and purpose is in direct alignment with your company.

Before You Continue

As we wrap up this stage (and before you go through the action steps), take a moment and imagine what life will look like when your Humble Alpha purpose is solid and you're living it fully. What does life look and feel like? How amazing does it feel to know exactly how to direct your focus on the most important things. How does it feel to know you've identified blindspots and know they won't hold you back anymore? Grab your bookmark, save this spot, and put this book down. Do this mental exercise and then continue to the action steps.

Action Steps

Congratulations on making it to the end of stage two! Before you take action on these steps, be sure you've completed all the action steps for stage one. It's vital you do the work on stage one before taking action below, because they all build upon each other.

Break the following action steps down into bite-sized steps. Some action steps will only take a few minutes, while some may take hours, days, or even weeks to solidify. Don't try to perfect these action steps. Take action and keep making progress. Do the work, take the next action, and let all the action steps in this book build on one another. You've got this.

Remember, action steps are things that are in your control; they are something you can do. They aren't outcomes, which are things outside of your immediate control. Here they are:

1. **Find Purpose** – Sit down for 1-3 hours and answer the questions below. In our book resources, we have additional questions to ask yourself. Break this action step into several sessions if needed.

   a. Known-Knowns

   b. Juice in Life

   c. Connecting the Dots

2. **Define Macro and Micro Purpose** – Take the answers from above and begin to define your purpose. This will likely take several sessions, so schedule them.

   a. Macro Purpose

   b. Micro Purpose

3. **Test Purpose** – This will be an ongoing practice, depending on where you are in your journey. Take what you defined in Step 2 and take action on it to see if it really resonates with you. Keep testing and refine your purpose until it is solid. Only by experience will you truly know.

4. **Direct Your Focus** – Your focus should only be on what your purpose is at this point. Don't waste time with things that aren't rooted in your purpose or identity. Create your focus cave and constantly remind yourself of your focus.

5. **Build Habits and Routines** – Restructure your day so you are habit stacking into your best self. Replace old habits with your newly defined habits that are in alignment with your new identity and purpose. At a minimum, build (or refine) the following habits and routines:

   a. Morning routine

   b. Evening/bedtime routine

   c. Replace all bad habits with new ones

   d. Create or refine your workout routine

   e. Start the bar very low and build from there.

6. **Identify Blind Spots** – This will happen throughout life, but you will begin now. Find someone to help you identify your blind spots. He or she can be a mentor, coach, or someone highly experienced in an area you know you need growth. Begin your outreach now. For this action step, pick 1-3 people who can assist you.

Be sure to set a deadline for each step, and for the entire steps 1-6 as well. This deadline will ensure you prioritize the action steps and make continual progress. A deadline isn't: "I'll have it done 2 weeks from now;" it's looking at the calendar right now, and setting the deadline for each action step. Make these action steps a priority in your life.

Bookmark this page to keep track of your next action step. You can also download this checklist, along with other worksheets, resources, and videos that help you dig deeper into these exercises. These bonuses are free of charge, and they come along with this book. To get them, go to: HumbleAlphaBook.com/bonus

EMPOWER

⌒⌒

"Treat people as if they were what they ought to be,
and you help them become what they are capable of being."

— Johann Wolfgang von Goethe

One cannot create a powerful organization, without distributing power throughout. The electrifying power you have within means nothing if you don't share it with those around you. Delegated power allows others to become the greatest version of themselves. Sharing power is paradoxical in nature, for true power is amplified when shared, not diminished.

In order to share power, and empower, you must see the potential in others to harness that power. Empowerment is entrusting power to others so they can do more, accomplish more, and innovate more than you could by holding onto it yourself. Empowerment, therefore, is creating the space for them to step into their greatness.

The Company as Ecosystem

You're the Architect, and Your Company is the Ecosystem

Think of your company as an ecosystem with you as the architect. Each part of your company, division, or team is an ecosystem you create that is self-sustaining, empowered, and capable of making decisions within their realm of influence within the company. You are the creator of that ecosystem; you set the stage and enable them to make decisions that make the company better.

You set the rules of the environment based on your identity and the game you're playing. Although you're setting the conditions, you won't create every system, process, or action. You actually empower your team to create them, because they likely know them better than you do. You will see how empowering that can be and what a different atmosphere it creates than when you micromanage your company and team. When you're a micromanager, you have to control everything. You want to know where everything is, and you want things done your way or the highway. Step away from the model of micromanagement, and think of your company in a new light. It's less exhausting for you and the people on your team.

When it comes to models of leadership, there is the empowerment model and the providership model. There's also the Seagull Model, which says to fly high at the macro level and drop white droppings on everyone. We don't necessarily like that approach. Who wants to go about their day and then—quite literally—get dumped on? The way we look at it is simple: Surround yourself with people who are more capable in their specific areas of expertise than you are. That's the first aspect of being the architect of your company's ecosystem.

When you ask yourself: *How do I build the best building?* You know you won't be the one out there with a hammer and nails (unless that's what you do). You're not going to say, *"I want to choose plastic because it looks better than steel."* You're going to find someone who knows about steel and plastic and what the differences are. If you think about your business(es), like an architect, you want to build the best foundation you can, so it will sustain the greatness and activity you build on top. Build your company for growth, and once you empower your team to grow, the sky's the limit (except in the case of Elon Musk, where it's not).

How to Empower People

You can empower people in many ways at every stage of their employment—from when you hire them and train them on daily activities and through daily interactions. You can implement appraisals or 360-degree feedback. It's as easy as heading to Google and searching for a list of ideas you can implement to empower your team. You'll come up with a list of great ways from several thought leaders and experts. In our companies, we like to have personal moments with everyone. There are many ways that I do that.

For almost 15 years, I was the Director of Operations for a company in Europe. We had about 3,500 employees in 87 locations across nine countries. It was a pretty big deal, and I was quite young at the time--around 33 years old. I had a U.S. military background, so my previous approach was "shut up, listen to me, and do your job." However, I'd spent about 4-5 years as an entrepreneur in the bar and nightclub business in Berlin, Germany. In the bar and nightclub business, you have to listen. You cannot micromanage a bar or nightclub; it's impossible.

You have to trust the people around you. Teach and train them, but then empower them, so they grow and take committed ownership of their tasks. In a bar, you always have a bartender who wants to please the guests, so he or she makes up cocktails and new drinks. You can do one of two things with that. You can say, *"Stop making up cocktails and stick to the menu,"* or you can say, *"Keep doing that, and we'll put them on the menu. We'll also enter them into a cocktail creation contest."* I chose the second approach and it not only kept my bartenders happy and creative, it kept the customers happy, too. It was this experience that taught me to go from *shut up and listen to me to let's do this thing together.* After that, when I stepped into the corporate world as the Director of Operations, I blew everyone away with the models I used.

The first thing I did when I took on the role of director was to interview people and create assessment centers—not the cheesy type—but the kind that uncovered information and provided insight. I had the employees debate one another about the best solutions to problems, and the process revealed several key insights.

At one point during my tenure in that position, I traveled to Zurich to one of the most successful locations. It had previously brought in about $1.5 million a month but recently had flatlined. Leadership wanted to break through that revenue ceiling, and they couldn't do it no matter what they tried. I helped them do it. I made regular visits and used the same team without firing anyone. How did I do it? What was the trick?

Whether you step into an existing or new company, you first need to make people aware that you are the new leader. They have to know there's a change beyond a new suit and tie walking through the halls. You need to change the team's perception of reality when you arrive. To do that, I rearranged the office. I put staff members where the boss used to sit and put the boss where staff members used to sit. I moved desks around to create islands or faced desks towards the door rather than a wall.

I created a kind of coworking space within the office. Then, I'd have them paint the office after-hours because it establishes teamwork; they're creating something new together. Making physical changes shows people you're not messing around. Although these are external activities, there's subtle internal work happening.

Next, I coached each person through their strengths. It doesn't matter if they're talented at art or they work at a gas station. You can always find a way to use their strengths to benefit your business. We'll touch on this later, but there are sixth essential human needs that come into play here.

At this European corporation, I became known as the turnaround guy. I did it over and over again. I went in, changed the office around, painted, trained the people, identified their strengths, and introduced what we called credo moments.

Once a day, we'd get together for a team meeting. Everyone had to say three things: what happened between this meeting and the last meeting, what was going to happen between this meeting and the next meeting, and the action plan for that. We'll go into that more in-depth later, but once I did the turnaround, I let the people at the business run with it.

You might wonder how you teach people to "run with it" and carry the torch. Let's talk through one example of how you teach someone to come up with solutions on their own rather than coming to you.

When people come to you with a problem, do not answer the question. Tell them to come up with three solutions they would stand behind. When they return to give you their three solutions, ask: *"Which one do you stand behind the most?"* They might reply with, *"Well, number two."* Then ask, *"Why?"* Once they tell you, then say, *"Okay, good! If you stand behind it, roll with it."*

The next time they come in with a problem, this process will go more quickly. The third time, they won't come to you with issues anymore, because they know what you'll tell them to do. To get someone to carry the torch, teach and empower them to look at problems from different angles, not just one. Try this yourself. Try to come up with three solutions to solve a problem you already know how to answer. It forces you to identify different ways to look at the problem.

That's just a quick overview. In our Humble Alpha Leadership Program, we dig more deeply into how to turn around businesses and empower teams without running yourself ragged, putting more on your plate, or having to hire and fire team members.

Providership

We define providership to mean we're not giving from an empty cup. We fill our cup first so that we can provide for other people from abundance rather than lack. Getting clear on your identity and purpose is a form of filling your own cup. From that position, you can support the six essential human needs (which we'll discuss later) of the people in your organization or on your team.

If you try to provide from an empty cup—with emptiness or a void inside— you won't be as effective, and people will sense the lack. How many times have you encountered a person who gives and gives while you see the pain and exhaustion in their eyes? They're hurting because they're giving from an empty place. This is why it's so essential to get clear on your identity and purpose.

Everyone has their own definition of what providership means. A father who's married to a stay-at-home wife may feel like he has to provide for her and their children. A mother who's married to a stay-at-home dad feels the same way. Providership is more than monetary provision, however. It's an attitude and mindset. At one of our retreats in Peru, we talked about providership and having an overflowing cup, and many people equated it with work and money.

When you fill your cup and see yourself as the top cup in a champagne tower that fills cups all the way down the pyramid, you understand what happens when the cup overflows. It automatically trickles to the other cups. This is the kind of providership we talk about. It's almost effortless because when you're at the top of your game as a Humble Alpha and filling your cup, providing for others is a byproduct. You overflow to everyone you come into contact with and create radiant value. People want to be near you, and they want what you have.

Providership is not about what you're doing on the outside; it's about what's going on, on the inside. Providership has an element of personal and professional development to it, so you can imagine what kind of extrapolated results and cascade effect happens if everyone in that champagne tower steps into their Humble Alpha and has overflowing cups.

The most valuable assets in any company are human assets. And every single one of them has needs. When you genuinely care about them as humans and provide for their essential human needs, you allow them to step into greatness towards the same unified vision.

Refining Your Company Purpose

The goal of every company is to be the best, most sought-after company to work for. Google has been a top company to work for, and people love it because they have ping pong tables and a Starbucks in its headquarters, but that wears off eventually. What doesn't wear off is learning, esprit de corps (a spirit of cohesion and success), and growth.

If you look at the military as an example, you can be in the Army, Navy, Air Force, or Marines for one year, but for the rest of your life, you're a marine, soldier, seaman, or an airman. Why? They drill this military identity into you. It's the esprit de corps.

A 4-Star General completed a study and wrote an article that discussed what could happen to the corporate world if it got the kind of cohesion and embodiment of values the military does. Have you ever heard anyone say that they're an IBMer or Appler because they once worked at IBM or Apple? No, that doesn't happen, but people develop an esprit de corps in the military. If you evoke this spirit in companies—even to a small degree in comparison to the military—they change. I've done this myself, and the results are magical. When this happens, everyone does what they're supposed to do because they know it's the right thing. Everyone leads toward the mission, vision, and value proposition because they understand what it is and what it means, and they helped co-created it.

Co-Creating a Mission

Co-creating a mission and vision statement is important. If you're an existing company, you don't have to start from scratch or hire a new team. We run a brand messaging workshop that helps companies truly identify their mission, vision, and value proposition. People don't think they need to put time and effort towards this beyond coming up with a catchy tagline. They want a memorable slogan like McDonald's "Loving it" and think that's all they need. A catchy tagline won't get anyone to peak success.

If you don't know what you do as a company, who you are, what your purpose is, or whether it aligns with your individual mission and vision, you won't hit your peak. If you don't know where you're going, how do you expect people to know and head in the same direction? You won't reach the customers, clients, or patients you're meant to reach because you don't know what you don't know. You won't see what you need to do on a larger scale.

For example, if I have a value proposition that says, "We build the only electric cars for speed-lovers that reach 0 to 60 in 5.2," that's very specific. I've implemented this branding workshop for $500-million-dollar companies that have been in business for ten years. We sit down, and they learn they have no idea who they're selling to, which shocks them. They thought they were doing a good enough job. It's not good enough. Your value proposition will change over time, so you have to revisit it continually.

On the flip side, one of the biggest problems early-stage businesses have is an incomplete vision, mission, or value proposition statement. They sell to everyone and haven't selected a market niche. It's easy to believe that the more people you talk to, the more you'll sell, but that's not true. That's a scarcity mindset in action.

Narrowing down a market does not mean narrowing down sales. Many new business owners think they need to talk to everyone, or they'll miss a client or customer, but if you speak to an individual and specifically address the problem you know that person has, he or she is going to come to you. Then you can serve him or her with other tools and resources. You don't have to talk about everything you do. You may be able to help everyone on the planet in some way, but that's not the point of going into business or driving your business forward. You have to speak one language to one demographic. That's providing a solution.

I did some work with an Austrian company with 14 health club locations. The owner was very successful, and he only had women working for him, which was interesting. All of the staff at every location were women.

He ran a women's health club chain, and they had an identity crisis. It was called heroine in English but a different word in German, which has a different sound and connotation. It embodied the idea of a female hero who attacks life every day.

When I stepped in, I asked: *"What do you mean when you say that they're heroine? Why are they heroine?"* They couldn't answer me, so we needed to work through that. After our session, they lit up. All of their staff members were at the meeting and we paired them up to come up with ideas of what it means to be a heroine. In the end, we came up with their mission, vision, and value proposition (as a company with all the staff). Around eight months later, they sold each location for more than the entire 14 clubs were worth eight months prior. Why? Because they knew who they were talking to, and they attracted those clients. They got free media coverage in the newspaper, and people saw something was different.

If you've identified those things from the beginning, you cannot imagine the power you have behind your company. If you're in a position now where you've flatlined (because a lot of people hit a revenue ceiling), revisit your mission, vision, and value proposition. Not too long ago, I had a client who couldn't breakthrough $150K per month. We revisited her messaging and who she talked to. We also looked at what solution she provided. Typically, that's all you need to do, and you'll break through that ceiling.

When you clearly define your vision and mission for your company, everyone in your organization can align with it. Whether it's new employees or current employees, they get clear on how they fit into the bigger picture of the company, which adds ten times the clarity to their roles. On top of that, applicants are automatically attracted to your company because they see exactly where you're going, what your mission is, and how they fit in.

Your team can enter into that mission because they know that every stroke of the pen—every move that they make—contributes to the bottom line and the achievement of that mission. When you're clear on your mission and vision, it automatically becomes the focus, and non-essential targets get laid aside. Your vision and mission hone everyone's focus because they can start to see the opportunities and identify how they can reach the vision faster, better, more efficiently, and more profitably. Remember when we talked earlier about focus? Now that focus isn't just you, it's amplified within your entire organization. How powerful is that?

Does that mean you need to have every single person in your organization involved when you create your mission, vision, and value proposition? When you have a corporation with 6,000 people, it's impossible. But, you can take the department heads.

I like to pull people from all areas. I pull a few people from upper management, middle management, lower management, and staff. One time, I even pulled in two people from the cleaning staff. It's important not just to pick your shining stars and the people you like, too. Make sure you choose people who are in the shadows doing their day-to-day jobs. Those are the people you want. You want to know precisely what they're thinking and why. The ripple effects of choosing all kinds of people within the company will say volumes to the entire company. It's a lot of work, and you might start the meeting in a suit and tie and end it in a t-shirt soaked in sweat, but it's powerful and incredibly insightful.

You set up the company to perform at its best by getting clear on your vision and mission. This allows for everyone to refine their individual roles and responsibilities; it helps you build your A-Team.

Building and Retaining an A-Team

The term A-team comes from the special forces—an acronym ODA, or Operational Detachment Alpha. You've probably seen the TV shows from back in the 80s or the movie *The A-Team*, which the show got it from the US Army Special Forces. In the real world, an A-team is a high performing team you can scatter throughout your organization. Each division or part of your company should be its own A-team. Part of the reason why high-performing teams work is that they're empowered, have high skills, and their character is par to none. You have to have that magical combination of top skills, character, and the ability for them to see how they fit into the bigger picture.

In the special forces, each person on the A-team is world-class in their area of expertise, and that's precisely what you want for your company. Use differentiated skill sets and roles so each person can take real ownership of their area. That's a part of the empowerment model because when you have real ownership, you're able to run as fast as you want. Each A-team member has those principles embedded in him or her, so it doesn't matter what that person does within the company, he or she will find a better way to do it.

To make it clear, your A-team is a very small, tactical, and strategic unit. Like in the special forces, you have a weapon's guy, demolitions guy, communications guy, medic, and the team leaders. Everyone has a task, and if that person doesn't do that task, the whole team falls apart. The responsibility is on your shoulders.

In a company with departments, you would have your marketing, sales, or human resources teams, and the specialists within make up your A-teams. You get the best people and players and keep those players by empowering them and allowing them to grow. Your A-team is growing your company for you. You won't have to ask them to do something; they'll come to you, present you with an idea, and ask if they can run with it. I've run companies like that where I've run myself out of a job because the A-teams just took over. They did a fantastic job and it was so much better than I could have done on my own. When your A-team doesn't exist, you can't reach the level you want to achieve on your own.

Meetings with Meaning

I've run meetings once a day for several years now where I bring in A-team members, and it's been so successful that the CEO of a company I consult for had me implement this in 87 locations in person. What you do is bring the entire A-team together, and when I say the whole team, I mean you find your A-players within part-timers, full-timers, contractors, the cleaning staff—everyone. Every A-team member has to be in that team meeting because you're talking about the vision and you want a five-minute-per-department overview. You don't want people to talk long, just an overview. I cut through all of the BS. Everyone needs to know in advance that this is a different kind of meeting. I call them "meetings with meaning."

In these meetings, talk about three issues: what key things happened between the last meeting and this meeting; what your plans, numbers, or growth goals are from this meeting to the next; and what your action plan is to achieve those goals. The leader of every department gives a rundown of these items. We also rotate leadership of the meetings, because it's very empowering and forces people to step into their greatness. It's as simple as that. It takes about five minutes per department, and you're getting a quick picture. If you need to discuss anything deeper than that, take it off to the side after the meeting in a one-on-one. Typically, the department will have one-to-one meetings once a week.

Once every department has gone through its quick overview, the whole team has a credo moment. You develop a credo for your team that comes from your mission, vision, and value proposition. For example, a credo we used in my previous role as Director of Operations for the European company was

"I inspire myself, I inspire my team members, and I inspire the world around me." They'd ask questions of themselves like: What do I do to inspire myself every day? What do I do to inspire my team and the world around me? Each day, one person had the task of presenting a credo moment, so if you have 30 members on your team, every 30 days, you're up.

These credo moments can be cheesy, exciting, or unique—it doesn't matter. For example, for one individual's credo moment, he told everyone in the meeting they had five minutes to go outside and speak to someone they hadn't spoken to before. They had to elevate that person and make him or her feel fantastic. Then they came back in and reported on what happened. It was amazing. If you want to experience the impact kind words and attention can have, this is a great exercise. Beyond elevating your A-team, this elevates your entire business because suddenly, you have 20-30 employees out there talking to staff, clients, and customers all at once. It just explodes.

At the end of these meetings, we'd usually linger around together. One of the guys created some Tai Chi movements, and we put our own words to it. We'd end with that. It was cheesy at first, and people were embarrassed, but in the end, it turned into our company culture, and we would use those words in passing to each other. You foster growth through small things that bring people together and make them want to be better. There are several meeting models that we go through, but this is an example of a basic approach that's very impactful.

Hiring People and Building the Team

When you build an A-team, attracting and hiring those highly-skilled, passionate, and driven people is a massive step in the process. There are two hiring philosophies out there, which broadly say you hire for values and train for skills or you hire for skills and screen for values. You'll approach this based on your value proposition, but we genuinely believe that skills can be trained. We always hire based on character. If you hire based on character, however, you have to conduct a different style of interview.

In a character-based interview, you empower the interviewee to create something for you and come up with ideas and solutions for problems you have in your business. You want to see what kind of character that person has. For example, if he or she has an attitude like "Why are you asking me this when I'm not working here yet? You're not paying me." Then, it's "See ya!" If someone sits down and says, "Well, let me think about it for a second. Do you have this?" If he starts asking questions about the tools he needs to solve this problem, you're looking at someone who has a character. Asking questions and being willing to give it a try is an indicator that you have someone who wants to commit, grow, and make this happen. When you do this, you'll find that your interviews are a lot shorter, and you'll have to do a lot more to find the right people because you no longer have checkboxes to follow. It's not necessarily what they do to attempt to solve it, but how they do it.

Another tool you can use when building your A-team is one that we call the Wow Test. How do you know when you have an A-player on your team? That person wows you every once in a while. He could be incredibly skilled at what he does, but then every once in a while, he wows you above and beyond what he'd typically do. Maybe he figured out a solution to a problem no one had identified yet or found an innovative way to do something that no one was even thinking about within the organization. That's one indicator that you have an A-player.

The more that individual does that, the more you know he is an incredible, high-performing person. You want to hire and keep people that continue to wow you. Think about the people on your team and ask yourself: How many people have wowed me with their skillset and character? The same test can apply to business partners or joint ventures, too. Heck, it can even apply to potential relationship candidates. Give them the Wow Test.

Organizations that have a clear vision and mission, along with a high-performing A-Team, have layers of depth that make it incredibly special and unique, and that depth is culture. Not just culture, but undeniable culture.

Building Undeniable Culture

If your organization has flatlined, building an undeniable culture will help transform it. If you're building a new organization, you can do this from the very beginning and be leaps and bounds ahead of your competition.

Earlier in this book, we mentioned rearranging offices and routines for organizations that had flatlined or needed a turnaround. Many people confuse an organization's physical space with its culture. Let's first discuss structure and culture. There's a difference.

Structure is related to rearranging offices and routines. It addresses the things you can move, see, and touch. This includes procedures and processes. The structure of a company involves things you can change immediately.

Culture takes time to cultivate. It's like a seedling that needs to grow into a plant. You need to know if it needs direct or partial sunlight or what kind of fertilizer it takes. You have to talk to it. The culture of a team never stops changing. It's a constant process, which means you have to continually focus on it. You have to be attentive all the time, but you can't do it on your own. This is why you need to have empowered people in place.

Your company culture is an intangible that ultimately creates the most significant return on investment for your company. It's also the most challenging investment to measure, but it's the most important one to put in place. Just remember, you can't create an undeniable culture overnight, but you can wreck it overnight. In fact, you can destroy it immediately.

Culture isn't the tangible things you can see from the outside, it's the sum of intangible things within. The things we see on the outside are a byproduct. We frequently refer to tangible, external things as the byproduct of something internal happening. It's the same thing with culture. You can't quite measure it like you can other measurables in the business.

You've heard of companies that add ping-pong tables, coffee shops, and massage parlors on their company grounds. Large organizations have done this with some success, but it only goes so far if there is no "internal" change of culture. They are simply putting a band-aid on a wound that will continually appear. What you want to do is go to the root of the problem, and that's the culture.

Your company vision and mission set the stage for the culture. The ecosystem you set up for the company is also a factor, as are the values of the company.

It can be difficult to change a company culture.. To make it easier, have a clear vision and make it meaningful for everyone in the organization. When people know that changes are happening for the betterment of all involved, it's much easier for them to not only comply but to take ownership of the cultural change.

The start of cultural change begins with you as the leader. That's why we focus on individual identity and purpose at the beginning of the book. Part of your identity is to be a clear communicator and live by what you say. If you want the company culture to change, you are the first example of that change. People will see that you're sincere, and they will follow suit.

Even though you, as the leader of the organization, will lead from the front, you also need to create "buy-in" from team members. Just as you do with creating the vision and mission with all (or key) team members, you can do the same thing with the culture. Create a survey for everyone to take and invite them to share suggestions. Take the best ones and decide as a team which ones to embed in the culture. Test some of the ideas during meetings and see where it goes. Be flexible and experiment with the culture, you may be surprised with what team members and employees come up with.

Empower already strong leaders to lead the charge on the company shift. This builds upon their already strong leadership, and it will be a positive sign from other team members that there's buy-in from more than just you at the top. Once many people have taken ownership of the change of culture, it is inevitable that others will want to be a part of it too.

The character of the team members will adjust to the culture you implement. New hires will automatically be assessed on how well they fit into the company culture. The more defined and stronger the culture, the easier it is to identify the right new hires.

Find natural ways to reinforce the company culture. We already discussed meetings and esprit de corps activities that the company can do. But don't stop there. Search out additional ways to embed the culture that resonate with your company in every capacity. You want the entire company to eat, breathe, and live the company culture to the bone.

One way to ensure a positive cultural shift is to create feedback loops. By finding ways to measure the culture, you can analyze the data and adjust from there. Know that you may implement the changes for the culture quickly, but the actual change in employee behavior may take longer. Keep at it and the culture will shift. The process of changing culture never seems to happen fast enough, but it is well worth the effort.

Another way to implement a positive company culture is to create goals based on the vision and mission of the company. You can also create a list of top-3 character traits of all team members. Embed personal development and Quality of Life training and activities and make them available to the entire organization. All these "intangibles" lead to powerful, tangible results.

When you get the company culture right, you create even more loyal team members and attract the right new hires. People are happier, performance increases, there is less stress in the workplace and, of course, revenue will increase. Building undeniable culture requires having conversations with the people in your company. You need a strategy that allows people to open up and step into their greatness. We know just the way. It's called Creating Space.

Creating Space

On the way back from one of our retreats in Peru, I flew business class. The airline upgraded me, and I sat with a friend who'd gone on the retreat with us. Someone came up from coach and sat down in a seat that wasn't his. The stewardess tried to get him to move, but he refused to budge. Then another stewardess and another tried. Finally, the captain of the plane came out to speak to him. The man said, "I'm not moving. I'm a person. I don't want to sit back there with all the cattle. I want to sit up here in peace." They explained to him that he didn't pay for business class so he couldn't be there.

A couple of minutes later, I saw the stewardesses up front taking off their ties and jewelry. I asked them what they were doing, and they asked me to help them put him in a headlock so they could handcuff him. They planned to land in Barbados—which was quite a detour—and arrest him. "Let me try to talk to him before we tackle him," I said.

I went up and kneeled down beside him. "I want to tell you, you've got the biggest set of cahoonas I've ever seen. What you're doing is amazing!" I said.

"Really?" he started laughing.

I went on, "Yeah, I've never seen this happen, and I fly all the time."

"I don't want to sit back there, man. It's so crowded. It's stinky. It's horrible. I hate it," he replied.

"Look, I get it. I want to sit up here too, but I can tell you this...they're going to land this plane in Barbados and arrest you, which is cool because I wouldn't mind spending some time there, but that's probably not the best thing for you right now," I said.

"I'm going to move," he said, and got up and left. The whole crew was shocked. The captain threatened arrest, but nothing moved him. What moved him was the space I created around him. I just let him step into his own greatness, and it allowed him to breathe."

That's creating space.

I walked up to him with no expectations. I didn't want anything from him; I just wanted to solve his problem. I intended to elevate him to solve the problem. He obviously didn't feel valued in his life. The crew didn't understand; they skipped the entire personal element and went right to the structural solution, which was to get him to move. Structural solutions don't always solve problems. He wanted to be there because he wanted to feel valued and appreciated.

One key component of that story is that I got down to eye-level with him. I actually learned that at TGI Fridays as a waiter, believe it or not. You get down on their level and meet people where they are. It doesn't matter if it's an emergency situation from Peru to Madrid or if it's having a one-on-one personal meeting with one of your team members.

One of the cornerstones to our Humble Alpha methodology, especially when it comes to empowering your team, is creating space. Creating space is a part of your identity. You have to ingrain it within you. Imagine creating space around every single person you encounter, so they can step into their greatness in that very moment.

You can create space around every person you talk to, whether it's an audience, small group, barista, or board of directors. Just by being aware of the concept of creating space, people change their state. This concept is all about seeing other people's potential. You can create space intentionally in a boardroom during a meeting or playfully and joyfully as you're joking around and having fun with people. The intention is to elevate others and help them take their next step towards greatness.

What's important to remember is that there is a difference between expectation and intention. We'll discuss this more in-depth later, but expectations involve our ideas around an end result, whereas an intention is the beginning of something. An intention is how we move forward towards the vision.

Creating space means that when I walk into a meeting, I see everyone there. I have no expectations or cookie-cutter solutions in my mind. I have a toolbox full of my knowledge, but I don't open the toolbox until the time comes. My only intention is to create value, and that means elevating the people in the room and finding a way to move them forward. I can tell you this—when you enter a meeting with that approach, you change the energy in the room. People step into that space.

What happens when two people come together in a neutral space? There's a third entity. That third entity is a mastermind. The word mastermind was made famous in the book *Think and Grow Rich* by Napoleon Hill. A mastermind occurs when two or more people get together, create space with each other, and come up with ideas and solutions they never could on their own. Science has proved that this happens, and it's incredible. In a mastermind 1+1 =11.

Previously, we wrote about how Steve Jobs got booted from Apple for aggressively competing against his own company. We mentioned that when Jobs came back, he did so not as a title, but as himself. When he came back, not only did he gain experience, but Jobs realized that to create the most amazing things that don't exist, he needed people he could motivate and inspire to create those things that don't exist. He created space for people. Jobs put them in place, empowered them, and truly let them step into their own greatness.

A famous comedian says Jobs stood on stage and said, "I did this," but he had a team of about 50 engineers behind-the-scenes who did it for him. What's very important to remember, however, is that he empowered them to create greatness. Other people slammed Jobs for taking credit, but his team was proud of him when he took the stage. They knew he was an empowering visionary. Jobs earned the credit, and his team wanted him to have it because he got them to a place they would never have been otherwise. That's the power of creating space.

Several years ago, I arranged a meeting with the world-famous tenor, Andrea Bocelli. I managed to arrange the meeting through one of his opening acts, a guitar duo called Carisma. I knew where Andrea was in his business and that he needed help. My only intention was to go into this meeting to meet Andrea and find a way to work for him. I would do this by adding value and solving problems, and I knew some of the problems he had.

I showed up at the meeting, but he wasn't there. His wife, Veronica, and her assistant, Alicia, were there in his place. They were both very Italian, and Veronica is a tiger. Nobody messes with her, not even Andrea (although he's very happily married with beautiful children).

Someone else might have walked into that meeting and been disappointed that Andrea wasn't there. I wasn't worried about it, and I had no fear. I wasn't nervous because my only intentions were to add value and solve problems.

We started talking, and they were surprised at some of the information I had. Veronica asked me how I foresaw us working together. I told her I'd like a retainer and a percentage of the deals I brought in. She literally laughed in my face and told me that no one in the music industry got retainers. I explained to them that I only worked that way, and it was up to them. I told them they needed to decide whether they required my solutions or not. I walked out with a contract for a retainer and commission.

I never once had to sell them. All I did was create space. Both Veronica and Alicia felt at ease with me, and I worked for two years for team Andrea Bocelli and absolutely loved it. This changed my life forever, and it all started because I embraced my Humble Alpha, created space, and remained resolute in my purpose.

When you create space around an individual, that person has room to expand and grow in your presence. It's like a shift. Imagine being on a crowded bus where you're restricted, and there's no room for you to move. You don't have space, and it's almost impossible to invite someone to sit next to you because there is nowhere for them. Creating space eliminates restriction; it invites possibility. It turns potentiality into actuality. As you create space around other people so they can expand, they also have greater space to invite others in. As often as you can, practice this intentionally and eventually, it will become your new default.

By its very nature, creating space is customized for each moment. Each moment calls for something slightly different. That's why a 'cookie-cutter' solution doesn't work. You're meeting people where they are, and going with them in the direction they are moving. Still, there are common elements and principles at work nearly every time you create space. In no particular order, they are:

- **Bring only intentions into the interaction, no expectations.** Intentions are how you begin the interaction. Expectations refer to how you want the outcome to look like.

- **See the potential in all those involved.** Don't see their past failures. Don't assume they will be 'less than ideal.' Know that with this interaction, they will be reaching their potential for this moment.

- **Create the space of openness and no judgement.** Lack of judgement automatically puts people at ease. You know the feeling of people being judgy, you always feel less open and less willing to share. Being judgemental is a deeply embedded attribute for many, so you will need to learn to let go.

- **Allow all to step into their greatness, even you.** With that openness you helped create, you have created the space for greatness to occupy. With everyone involved reaching their potential and stepping into their greatness, everyone will be better off after this interaction. Just as the Humble Alpha and greatness are within you, so they are in all those around you.

- **Meet them where they are.** As a Humble Alpha, you may have things in life 'figured out.' Because of that, it can be easy to give answers and lay out the 'entire path.' Creating space is only about the present moment, helping them take the very next step.

- **Provide value.** Because you are showing up wholly and fully for that person in front of you with no preconceived notions or cookie cutter solutions you are allowing power to flow towards the only one thing you actually have control over: your intention of providing value. That value can be an innovative solution, lending an ear or a warm smile. Whatever the moment calls for, that's the value you bring to the table.

- **Be present.** Subtle nuances will trigger insights. Small gestures or words will spark ideas. Your intuition will lead to the next question you ask. This can occur when you are fully present. Don't allow distractions to derail a potentially powerful experience.

- **Go with the flow.** You may lead the conversation, but you do it with power, not force. Being forceful and overwhelming will detract from the interaction. Lead, but with your Humble Alpha power.

This may seem like many principles, and you may have to hone each element with practice. Eventually, they will become second nature and you won't have to think about them. They will be part of your identity.

There are two primary ways to create space. The first is by doing it without any explanation to anyone. You create space, amazing things happen, people feel great talking to you, and you go on living your life. This will be the majority of your interactions in life.

The second way is to create space while intentionally bringing up the subject. You may do this in your meetings, brainstorming sessions and during masterminds, for example. The awareness you bring into the interaction powerfully shifts the energy of the room. People alter their state both consciously and subconsciously. The conscious awareness elevates their spirit and makes them feel good. They want to step into their greatness. People are aching for people to see the potential in them, their light. And you always do, with every person you meet.

The conversation opens up and you both share things that aren't normally shared, especially with those you previously didn't know well. Their body language will be more open. They'll lean in towards you. You'll notice more eye contact, more engagement. And it's not just them, your body language and openness will be reciprocal.

Their subconscious is affected as well. They notice subtleties, their senses heighten, and it's much easier to remain in the present moment because it's a great feeling. The mastermind is created and revelations become the norm. We believe this is how human interactions are meant to be experienced.

Time will fly and incredible things will happen naturally, without having to force anything.

When the moment is coming to a close, both won't want it to end. The feeling is great, the value is apparent, and all parties are better off because of it. You helped create the special moment. But don't be confused, it wasn't just you. It takes two to tango. It may be true that you are leading, but the synchronised dance was because all involved chose to dance together. Be proud that you set the wheels in motion. You led the way. You created space, and that space you created was greatness.

Macro and Micro Innovation

If innovation is part of your culture, it needs to happen everywhere. We break innovation down into macro and micro. Macro innovation begins with the CEO, business leaders, and the executive team. From their position, they bring innovative ideas and solutions for the overall vision and mission of the company. Often, this is done in broad strokes. It's big vision work.

Innovation also happens at the micro-level, and that's where individuals, team members, and departments find innovative macro or micro solutions for macro or micro problems they encounter in their day-to-day operations. By understanding that innovation can happen anywhere, you have this culture of empowerment where individuals within the company almost go from a bottom-up direction and innovate. They bring forth ideas to implement that allows for innovation to happen anywhere within the company.

The Humble Alpha has to be humble enough to allow those around him to grow and thrive by presenting innovative ideas and solutions. I have a client who is on his way to becoming a Humble Alpha. When someone presents a problem, he schedules a board meeting with all of the employees and puts the problem on the table. He always has a solution in his mind, but 5 out of 10 times, that solution is no longer valid after he hears his employees. This guy runs an eight-figure company, and he does this once a week. That's what it takes to break through revenue ceilings, have a global brand that's bigger than you see and reach, and create space around individuals.

When you're a Humble Alpha you carry this intrinsic value —this internal power—it's an attitude that you have, and you are like a nuclear power plant. When you go somewhere, you carry it. You carry it when you're the person who listens at a networking event or at meetings and allows other people to come up with ideas because you don't need to. You don't need to come up with an idea so you can stroke your ego or affirm yourself. Sure, you can come up with great ideas, and you do (otherwise, you wouldn't be where you are), but you know your power is in no way thwarted when someone else comes up with a better solution than you. You allow others to step into their greatness and discover things about themselves instead of telling them.

Unleashing your Humble Alpha is so fantastic because it touches every aspect of your life. It's incredibly powerful when you can sit somewhere in full confidence, knowing that by saying nothing until it's time, you're empowering the person across from you to grow and to thrive. For many people, this is unfathomable. It's counterintuitive at first glance because it's the opposite of what we've all been taught as leaders. We're supposed to lead. We have plans, knowledge, and wisdom. We're not saying you shouldn't have the knowledge or wisdom; you must. We're saying you need that tool-box, and you need to know when to open it up and when not to.

When it comes to macro and micro innovation, you guide and encourage your team, but you also inspire them to step up on their own. When your team members step up and look for solutions that make sense and your executive team is looking outward for examples to bring in, there's this culture of constant innovation. Many organizations put "innovation" on a pedestal. Avoid that and just focus on improvements, big or small, because innovation is a result of your team stepping up. This is excellent for your organization because the marketplace (and the world) is an uncertain place. The more you can create certainty within yourself and your organization because you are at the cutting edge of innovation—of solving problems and creating—it transforms how you serve your customers and the level at which you play in the marketplace. It's the whole concept of radiant value, which we touched on earlier but will go into more detail about later on.

Macro and micro innovation is a critical component of an organization. Apart from having all of the benefits we mentioned, it also increases productivity so you can scale your company. Innovation is what every single company looks at when they're looking at scaling, improving productivity, or decreasing conflict.

The Art of Communication

How does everyone know that innovation is an integral part of your culture? The art of communication plays a role here. There must be no assumptions regarding innovation or the culture of your company. Leaders can eliminate assumptions and bring clarity by having individual, one-on-one meetings. Group meetings are important, but having that one-on-one connection is vitally important. Depending on what the culture is in your company, you may have weekly, quarterly or annual one-to-one meetings.

When you're in the meeting, begin by creating space as we talked about before. Communicate the role you play and your responsibility as a leader. Lay out what you expect of them in their role and what their responsibilities are. Everyone needs to be on the same sheet of music. Ask them to share, from their perspective, what your roles and responsibility means to them. Part of the conversation around roles and responsibilities is bringing up innovation. Mention that you're empowering everyone within the company to bring forth innovative ideas and invite them to be part of that culture. It's direct, clear, and explicit.

Communication becomes art when no assumptions are present. A lot of companies want to innovate—every company wants to improve—but they don't make innovation an explicit part of the way the company operates. They try to do it themselves by forcing it from their fingertips. We talked about how Steve Jobs needed innovation, but he couldn't do it himself; he had to empower the people to do it for him while being very clear about what he needed.

Even if you can innovate yourself, is it really the best way? You shouldn't do it alone, because—as the following example illustrates—your team's insight and experience may foster a more innovative solution than you can come up with on your own. Going back to my example of a client of mine, remember what he said? When he walks into a meeting to address a problem, he always has a solution in mind, but 5 out of 10 times, it becomes irrelevant because his team comes up with a more innovative solution. That's 50% of the time. As the leader, why would you make a decision when you have many people who can give you feedback and oftentimes come up with a better solution because they're more familiar with the problem and your customers. You want to get all of that information.

Innovation needs to be co-creative. It should involve everyone at macro and micro levels. A CEO who doesn't know marketing may know the principles or have a broad understanding, but they don't know the intricate details around what makes marketing really good. With macro innovation, the CEO can bring forth the need to address the marketing and help direct innovation, but it's the marketing team who innovates on a micro-level. This sounds very basic yet a leading complaint from department heads and teams is that they cannot innovate and are only ever expected to execute.

To empower others and weave innovation into the fabric of the company, you will need to let go of certain things. Depending on your previous style of leadership, control, and management, you may need to let go of a lot. Luckily for you, we have the solution to teach you how to let go.

Letting Go to Empower

Once you know your mission, vision, value proposition, and that you want to create a culture of innovation, you know where you want to go. The next problem leaders face is how to get there. Many have identified where they want to go, but don't know how to get there, or they force it using old methodology. That's dangerous.

Earlier in the book, I touched on what you should do if a team member comes to you with a problem. You ask them to come up with three solutions they could stand behind and get back to you. They may think they only need one solution and get a bit irritated that you asked for three, but here's why you want them to dig deeply. You want them to get into the habit of doing research and finding different ways to solve the same problem according to their experience in their specific position. In the end, they are the ones who have to deliver solutions to the client directly. They need to be able to own it. No one wants to say to a customer "My boss said we have to do this."

What this does is create a dynamic between the parties involved.. You're creating a cohesive connection with a client that's going to stay with you longer because he or she sees that you're working together rather than getting dictated answers from a boss with whom they haven't established a personal connection or basis for trust.

This is much deeper than not asking the person who comes to you with a problem three questions (one of which isn't a question at all; it's more instructional). To review, the three questions you ask are:

1. Give me three solutions to the problem that you can stand by—The first time they do this, they may think they can only come up with

one, but tell them to do some research, Google, consult someone smart on the subject, or whatever it takes to find three solutions and report back.

2. Which one do you stand behind?—They may ramble a bit or say they also have a fourth one. Get them to tell you which one they stand behind.

3. Why do you stand behind it?—Get them to identify their why. Then, tell them to go make it happen.

As we mentioned before, the next time he comes back, do the same thing. The next time he comes to you, he'll likely be prepared and shoot off his three solutions and which one he stands behind. At some point, he'll probably ask whether or not he needs to come to you anymore to run the solutions past you. There you go; you have an empowered team member. Someone like that could turn into an invaluable team member because you're continually creating space to come up with new solutions.

What if the solutions to the problem are terrible or a person is afraid he or she will make a mistake? How do you handle that? Every leader knows how to coach. Coaching is asking questions, and you ask questions to keep the individual thinking inside the boundaries. For example, when they tell you why one solution is better than the other two, you may say, " Well, have you thought about this or that, or have you thought about what happens when this happens?" If the individual's response is no, tell them to see what he or she can find to cover that concern and come back. This is a coaching process. The first time might take longer, but each time it takes less and less time until it doesn't happen at all. You have to make time to do that deliberately. You're extracting their greatness via questions, and you, as the Humble Alpha, have to be patient during this process. It takes patience and a little bit of time upfront, but consider all of the time you're saving over the lifetime of your company by empowering your team members to come up with their own solutions.

If you want to solve company or customer problems, you don't just want to hand out solutions. You want to solve problems because that builds relationships and trust. You want every member of your team to be able to build relationships and trust with each other, clients, and the world at large. It's all about the human-to-human element.

When it comes to making mistakes, you have to allow your team members to make some mistakes. Of course, like when bowling with the bumpers, you want to keep them within the boundaries of making mistakes by coaching them, but they have to make mistakes to learn. Theory is great, but experience and applied knowledge is more powerful.

When your direct leaders experience the power of the 3-solutions rule, they will begin to implement it within their own team. You won't have direct one-to-one with everyone in the company, but you can embed this empowerment tool into the company culture.

If you ask anyone about the mistakes they've made, whether it has to do with business, performance, or personal situations, they almost always remember their mistakes. They'll touch on the mistake, but then they almost always talk about the lesson learned. If you're working with high-performers with great character who have caught the vision and know exactly where the company is going, they're going to learn from their mistakes and not repeat them.

Thus far, we've discussed much about providing others with what they need and meeting them where they're at. But how do we know what they need? Is there a model to help guide us?

Six Essential Human Needs

We humans have needs that can range anywhere from thousands of needs to beyond. These needs can be boiled down to six fundamental categories. Cloe Madanes introduced and Tony Robbins popularized this concept. Some are biological needs for survival, and some are emotional needs for feeling satisfied and happy in our lives. Understanding and applying the six essential categories of human needs to the way that you manage your team can improve your relationships and stimulate massive impact. As you read this book and embark on your Humble Alpha journey, you're fulfilling these six essential human needs for yourself, which makes you more capable of providing for other people. We discuss these needs in this section because they provide a necessary framework for empowering your team.

The six essential human needs are certainty, uncertainty, love/connection, significance, growth, and contribution. Picture a pyramid, with the basic needs at the bottom, laying the foundation for the remaining needs. The first four needs of certainty, uncertainty, love/connection, and significance are essential for human survival. The other two—growth and contribution—are essential for the spirit. The human needs we discuss first are at the bottom, which means people have to have these met before moving upward into other areas.

Certainty and Uncertainty

Certainty is comfort. It's the idea that we want to avoid pain and feel safe. We want to feel comfortable in our environment and feel a sense of security. For example, you want to know where your next meal is coming from, that you have a job, and that someone will care for you when you're sick. These examples demonstrate the positive side of certainty needs. Needing certainty also means you're more risk-averse and don't necessarily like change. People who need a lot of certainty often think they should stay as they are; they want to keep their security. In Germany, an organization conducted a poll and asked people what was more important to them: freedom or security. Most people said security; they preferred to feel secure and certain rather than uncertain.

The next essential human need is uncertainty, which is also known as variety because uncertainty has negative and positive elements. Variety can be considered a type of positive uncertainty. Everyone needs a measure of uncertainty or variety in his or her life. The mind and body require uncertainty. Think in terms of surprise or suspense. We need the excitement that comes from variety to stay alive. Who doesn't like the variety of travel or new experiences? Variety is a positive component of uncertainty. The negative part might be, for example, the uncertainty in being self-employed if, perhaps, you don't have money next month.

Certainty and uncertainty play off of each other. That's why we like to discuss them in pairs; every two work together and balance each other. For example, as an entrepreneur, how do I gain certainty that I'll earn revenue in my uncertain work on a joint venture? Maybe I collaborate or get a side gig until the joint venture is profitable. However, the rush and uncertainty of the venture itself is pretty thrilling. Certainty and uncertainty, along with significance and love/connection, are all personality needs.

Everyone has a different balance among these fundamental needs, and this is especially true for certainty and uncertainty. It's going to take some experimentation as you move through life to find that perfect balance for yourself. Balance for you may be different from balance for another person. Some people are adventurous and like variety. Other people like a secure lifestyle with just a sprinkle of adventure. You will discover your balance. Consider this idea of balance within your team members as well, because people have different levels of need, and you want to be mindful of that dynamic and offer your solutions according to those needs. Understanding the six essential human needs is a very powerful tool as a leader.

When you look at these essential needs, look at the flip side, too. When you see disruption in your team, you can review these needs. Is this person looking for certainty? If it seems like it, does he or she feel uncertain because a huge product launch flopped? The certainty in the company might be less secure because people are questioning: What now? This is where you have to step right in and give them certainty. It only takes a few words to affirm direction. Pull them aside or call a team meeting, and give everyone certainty.

Love/Connection and Significance

Significance is the need to feel special and important. Everyone needs to feel like they're doing meaningful work. Meeting this need for significance is where you, as a Humble Alpha, can help them take ownership of their roles and responsibilities so they feel proud that they are contributing to the company.

If you have someone on your team who is being loud and putting other people down, it's because he's seeking significance (or certainty or both). As a Humble Alpha leader, provide for that need. Call him up to the front of the room and have him present his numbers and give him an attaboy. He'll quiet down and be ready to roll.

Love, or connection, deals with a person's needs for unification, communication, or attachment. It's the need to connect with the human element. As a Humble Alpha, it's important to provide space for that connection. Everyone's style will be different, but you could have an open-door policy that allows anyone to speak with you. You can also provide space within your company culture where people can connect. We know that a baby who's not held and loved by his parents will die; that's how important love or connection is. When you see people stressed at work, it's either because they don't feel connected to the leadership or other members of the team, or they need significance, security, or variety. This is why it is so important to take the pulse of your team through one-on-one meetings and daily contact. The change in a person might appear subtly even though it can have massive impact. Knowing each person can help you assess their needs with more accuracy.

Significance involves our need to be a part of something and to do something great. It's our need for validation, approval, and honor. We achieve significance through being honoured or by achieving something meaningful. That's why creating company goals (in alignment with the vision and mission) are great for fulfilling the significance need. The second (and negative way) to achieve significance is to put someone down. Of course, we don't advocate that, but you see it all the time. If you have a team member calling someone an idiot or ugly or whatever, it's because that person is seeking significance. People will say it's jealousy, but it's typically not jealousy. That individual wants some honor and validation.

If you notice team members feeling disconnected or they're isolating themselves, what should you do? You might have a massage therapist come in once a week and offer massages to destress, do lunch or dinner together once a month, go to sporting events, or a hundred other activities which require connection. Sometimes words are enough and incredible breakthroughs happen in a one-on-one when you truly care.

You build significance and connection into your company culture by creating space and letting go to empower. This stage of empowerment creates connection within your team. People will become more helpful to one another and start collaborating on projects much more easily.

No matter where I worked, I rented an apartment upstairs above the office. I didn't like driving to work regardless of the country I was in, so I made sure I didn't have more than a 12-step commute. Having a fireman's pole would have been better. Occasionally I'd head up the stairs to my apartment and cook my mother's famous three-cheese stuffed pasta shells. I'd then head back down to the office and serve the team lunch.

Servant leadership provides an excellent framework for meeting the love and connection needs of your team. People knew I really cared, and I always made lunch or dinner about making a personal connection. Leaders look at this idea and say, *"I run a $25-million-dollar company. I don't have time for that shit."* Well, that attitude is why you're mad and frustrated, and probably why you're not running a bigger company.

Growth and Contribution

When we stop growing, we die. We need constant growth. We need to develop emotionally, intellectually, and spiritually. You have to cultivate and expand anything you want to maintain in your life, whether it's money, health, relationships, or happiness. People in your company must feel like they're growing emotionally and intellectually. Their relationships must grow, and it helps if their salary increases, too. They want to feel smarter and feel like they're gaining significance through what they're doing.

Growth and contribution are needs of the spirit, so contribution goes beyond one's own needs to give to others. People can contribute knowledge, money, help, advice, etc. Giving to others may mean giving time to community service, making a charitable donation, planting trees, writing a book, or giving to their children. Everyone can contribute in some way, and contribution is essential for a sense of fulfillment and happiness.

How can you get your employees to contribute to the bottom line? By clarifying your vision and mission and by empowering them to contribute in meaningful ways. It is also essential to their sense of fulfillment and happiness within your company. Google, for example, used to (and may still) let their employees work on any service project they wanted to for half a day a week. It was totally up to them. This perk had so much appeal and allure because people contributed based on their version of what contribution looked like.

Looking at this from a 360-degree angle, the goal is to view everything we talk about as a component of a larger system. These are essential needs, and understanding them helps you provide for those in your life enterprise—your team, family, and friends.

When you watch to see how your team interacts, stay aware of these needs. These needs will change so strive to recognize those changes. One day, a person might feel significant, and then, suddenly, he might be having trouble at home and no longer feel that way. He may come to work and need some empowerment, connection, love, or attention. Be open to noticing the subtleties. The only way to notice that is to know your team. You get to know your team by empowering them, working with them one-on-one, and going through the coaching process.

Before You Continue

As we wrap up this stage (and before you go through the action steps), take a moment and imagine what life will look like when your company is on fire with a clear vision and mission moving forward. What does life look and feel like? How amazing does it feel to have an A-Team performing at their highest every week? How does it feel to know you've empowered your team and innovation happens at every level of the company? Grab your bookmark, save this spot, and put this book down. Do this mental exercise and then continue to the action steps.

Action Steps

Congratulations on making it to the end of stage three! Before you take action on these steps, be sure you've completed all of the action steps for stages one and two. It's vital that you do the previous work before taking action below, because they build upon each other.

Break the following action steps into bite-sized activities. The majority of these action steps will likely take days or weeks to implement, and it may take even longer to see results. Trust the process. Changing your organization will take time. Take action and focus on small incremental progress. Do the work, take the next action, and let all of the action steps in this book build on one another. You've got this.

Remember, action steps are things within your control. They are something you can do. They aren't outcomes, which are things outside of your immediate control. Here are your action steps for this stage:

1. **Define/Refine Company Purpose** – Sit down with key team members or your entire company (if it makes sense) and refine your company vision, mission, and value proposition.

   a. Vision

   b. Mission

   c. Value Proposition

2. **Build Your A-Team** – Begin to empower all members of your team so they can step into their greatness, reach their potential, and become the A-Team you know they are capable of.

a. Restructure your meetings to reflect our "Meetings with Meaning" structure.

b. Add credo and team building activities into every meeting.

c. Try out the "Wow Test" on your current team members and see how you can cultivate that more.

3. **Create Undeniable Culture**

a. Ensure your company vision, mission, and value proposition is clearly communicated to every single person in the company.

b. Empower already strong leaders to lead the charge in any cultural changes.

c. Communicate to all team members that innovation is everyone's responsibility.

4. **Practice Creating Space** – Practice creating space with every person during every interaction you have. Over time, you won't have to think about creating space, you just will. It will become a part of who you are.

5. **Let Go to Empower** – Your involvement in the company should be very intentional. Allow the A-Team to step up and become empowered to make the company better, all while you tighten your focus on what you do best.

a. Establish the 3-solutions rule throughout the entire company.

6. **6 Essential Human Needs** – These are critical not only for your team, but for yourself. This action step is to learn about them conceptually, then begin to look at your team members one by one and how you can help fill those needs.

Be sure to set a deadline for each step, and for the entire steps 1-6 as well. Several steps will be ongoing and can happen simultaneously. Keep making progress and witnessing the gradual rewards. Make these action steps a priority in your life.

Bookmark this page to keep track of your next action step. You can also download this checklist, along with other worksheets, resources, and videos that help you dig deeper into these exercises. These bonuses are free of charge and come along with this book. Get them by going to HumbleAlphaBook.com/bonus.

Section Four

MOMENTUM

⌒⟶

"Great acts are made up of small deeds."

– Lao Tzu

One cannot become great by waiting on the sidelines for greatness to happen. Each small moment is an opportunity to build momentum towards greatness. Momentum is built day by day, interaction by interaction, person by person. It takes consistent action to yield the reward of greatness.

The intentions of your small deeds are of most importance, not the expectations. Act without expectation and know the reward will return to you. Bring the intention of value and elevating others into every interaction. Investing in others in small ways every day will build the momentum in ways you could never imagine.

Relational Capital

Investing in relational capital involves many concepts we've already discussed, such as letting go to empower others, creating space, and fostering a culture of innovation. Investing in relational capital asks the question: How do I elevate someone who is five managers below me? You elevate him and invest in him by listening, asking questions, and making him feel acknowledged. Simply doing that meets the human need for significance. This all ties together.

If you're a CEO or company owner whose company has grown significantly, your people still want to have contact with you. There's a level to which you must separate yourself to stay in the macro, but that doesn't mean certain people can't approach you. If a lower-level manager comes to you and asks how things are going or has a question, don't brush him off or tell him to ask his line manager. When the CEO or owner is suddenly untouchable, it erodes the esprit de corps, innovation, and open culture. It's your Humble Alpha thread that weaves through the entire company to foster innovation and productivity and decrease conflict. People still need to run their fingers across it.

The same thing goes when you're networking. How do you become the one person in the room whom everyone wants to talk to when you walk in? You listen, ask questions, acknowledge, and elevate. You have to be a great listener; that's what makes everyone want to talk to you because you're the only one listening. Everyone else is talking and handing out business cards, which is a simple example of a relational capital fail. Back in the day, I'd walk into a networking event and invest in people as human beings. I listened more than I talked. I asked questions and only talked about my business briefly.

In a networking event, let people talk about their business or whatever they want. You're there to provide value by creating space, listening, and then only giving the solutions to the problems or challenges that they share. That's investing in relational capital. Do this in all areas of your Life Enterprise. Leave people in a better place than when you met with them.

Relational capital is important because it's one of the only investments where you'll ever make a guaranteed return. Now, here's the key. Your return on investment might not be tomorrow; it might not be the next day. It could take 1 year or 15 years. And it might be from someone totally unrelated to the "initial investment."

Back in 2004, I was dating a member of the German Royal Family. Her job was to attend balls and open them as tradition dictates the highest royal opens with a Walz, so I learned to waltz and met many exciting people. I was a Humble Alpha and I dominated in every realm of my life. I could walk into any room and know who I was and wasn't because I'm clear on my identity and purpose as we discussed in chapter 1, whether I was speaking to a crown prince or the service team at the ball. That's why it's so important that you know who you are outside of your title and why we focus on it in such depth.

Eleven years before that, I was a soldier in the US Army. Suddenly, I stood with German royalty and was invited to royal weddings and birthday parties for the crown prince or king of such and such. I knew them all, and they treated me like one of their own. Why? Because I knew who I was. I wasn't trying to be anyone I wasn't. I wasn't trying to impress, and they valued that, even though they didn't necessarily know what I did or didn't do. They knew I was authentic, and I didn't bullshit.

I had a good time everywhere I went, and they may have thought I was a little goofy, but I was myself. Being authentically me got me a lot of influence in the world. I was powerful in my own space, personality, and identity. My purpose was absolutely clear. You'll get to this place as a Humble Alpha, too.

One day in 2004, I was at a ball in Paris when I met a 4th or 5th generation family bank owner. The Belgium banker was quiet, so I cracked a joke, as I usually do. Like a typical American, I didn't know how to keep my mouth shut. He started laughing, so I kept laying it on until we were laughing like two teenage girls; everyone looked at us and wondered what was going on. We had such a great time that night that we stayed in touch every two years or so. We'd send a text message or an email. Just recently, a project out of my scope came up, and I thought he might be interested. I called him up, and he wasn't, but he had something for me. There you go. We're still talking 15-20 years later. His wealth doesn't consume me. To me, he's a cool guy who is authentic and fun to be around.

The key takeaway here is that wherever you are—at a ball or business event—don't just walk around collecting business cards or trying to insert yourself into conversations. Be powerful in your own right and invest fully and wholly in the people right in front of you. Go in with no expectations but to provide value by creating space, listening, and then offering advice and solutions as people tell you about their problems. Give what you have and, eventually, you'll receive what you don't have in return. It's the law of reciprocity.

Just for a moment, think back on the networking events you've attended. Were you powerful in your own right? Did you feel out of place and not exactly sure what to do? Were you just trying to collect business cards and connections? When you implement this book and become a Humble Alpha, you'll notice the difference especially during networking events. You'll feel your own power. Every step will be filled with purpose. The purpose is to be who you are and provide value every step of the way, because that's just who you are.

When I started doing this consciously, I wanted to see how long it took to see returns and get to a point where I said, "Wow, I can't believe this is happening." It took a while; sometimes a year or more until I thought, Oh wow, that came out of nowhere or that client met someone who met someone because I invested in him or her. Those returns could look like a six-degrees of Kevin Bacon return on investment. The return might come directly from the person or relationship you invested in or it could come from the person in front of the person. You never know how it's going to ripple, and you can't expect that it will, so it's always a pleasant surprise.

There's an idea out there that if you have no expectations, you can never be disappointed, but that doesn't apply to every aspect of life. Either you have an expectation and verbalize it, or you don't have an expectation period. That goes for your relationships too. If you're a husband who comes home with flowers thinking, maybe tonight's the night, your wife feels that energy, but you're not saying anything or making a move. She sees you looking at her and wonders why you're looking at her like that. Do you want "it"? Do you not want "it?" The next thing you know, you're fighting about the toothpaste because the expectations aren't clear, and your intentions aren't aligned.

Radiant Value

I do a daily Facebook live video called *The Daily Purge.* I also post it in a closed, veteran's group of 14,000+ Military Veterans—called the Vetpreneur Tribe—that we run. I always talk about radiant value and creating space or something business or relationship-oriented. One of the members watches my videos with his son. One day, I talked about how to start your own business, seven ways to make immediate revenue, etc. This 8-year-old kid started to pick up on what I share.

His father reached out and told me that his son is an entirely different person. He's turning into a businessman. He meditates in the morning or tries to follow my morning routines. Every single day when he starts his day, he's positive and energized. This kid is changing his family, and it began with seeing my videos over the shoulder of his father, who I didn't know was watching. There are a lot of people out there who are watching. They might not comment, but they're there. That's radiant value, and it's amazing when you get glimpses of it.

As a Humble Alpha, when you elevate others, create space, invest in relational capital—everything we talk about in this book— you automatically create radiant value. It's a byproduct.

Remember, radiant value is the idea that as you deposit into one person, he deposits into another who deposits into another, and it moves through people. You create ripples of radiant value because you changed a life for the better, which means that person will more positively influence everyone around him. From there, it continues to ripple and ripple.

Radiant value is something you don't always see immediately. For example, we just asked a current client who's starting his journey to become a

Humble Alpha how he heard about us. He said he talked to a guy in Israel and helped him out, and that guy told our current client about us. I don't remember the guy in Israel that I helped. It was probably one of those things like, "Hey, I heard about you. Can we talk?" and we likely lined up a one-hour coaching session.

I had a massive impact on this guy to the point that he told other people about it. Our client heard about us, went to LinkedIn and contacted us. Now, if that's not radiant value through investing in relational capital, I don't know what is.

Radiant value always involves tangibles and intangibles. Sometimes, you experience the impact first-hand and feel the significance. Other times you don't know what kind of impact you had. On the flip side, radiant value is also tangible. Investing in relational capital has an impact on your revenue, customer loyalty—everything.

Radiant Value and the Need for Contribution

You can also tie radiant value to the human need for contribution. When you help someone contribute, you can turn around their state of mind and heart. If I have a day where I'm not in the groove, and I can't get out of my funk quickly like I typically do, I call up an old client I haven't talked to in a while. I'll ask that person what problems he or she is facing and contribute, contribute, contribute. I feel fantastic after that, and I'm ready to go. If I'm in a funk and need to contribute, I typically help a current or past client before I start with a new client.

Networking and Rapport Building

Networking is an overused and misunderstood concept. The traditional networking approach is cringe worthy. You have a name tag that says, *"Hi, I'm Billy,"* a stack of business cards in a shiny business card holder, and you're playing the game based on how many business cards you can collect and how many people you can impress. When I see that guy in a polo shirt and a pair of khakis coming toward me, I head in the opposite direction.

Meet Them Where They Are

When it comes to networking, we start at the very beginning, and that's meeting people right where they are. You can't come in too high or too low. You have to address them in a way that they're accustomed to. Meet them where they are, fit into the situation at hand, and be a listener.

Author and Storybrand Founder, Donald Miller, has it down pat. He recommends a concept called PPR, which stands for problem, product, and resolution. When someone asks you what you do, don't talk about yourself because most people ask what you do as a conversation starter. Most people launch directly into their 30-second elevator pitch, but that's 28 seconds more than I (and most people) can listen to. This happens all of the time. I say, *"Hey Tom, what do you do?"* and Tom launches into a long spiel. Two seconds in, I'm looking over my shoulder wondering where the cocktail waitress is.

If you use Donald Miller's system—PPR—when someone asks you what you do, you say, *"You know how CEOs work hard to rise to the top but often lose their identity in the process? When they go home at night and aren't "boss," they don't know who they are as a person or how to engage with their family. Well, we have a program called the Humble Alpha Leadership Program that addresses that challenge, resulting in an epic leader who dominates in all aspects of life—which is what we call "Quality of Life."* That's problem, product, and resolution. It's 10 seconds, and I'm completely done. By asking a question and introducing a problem before you lead into your product, people invariably nod in agreement that they're familiar with that challenge, because you've involved them in the explanation.

Then, I throw it back. For example, I might say, *"You said you have a trucking company in Boise, Idaho..."* and continue to listen. That person is now clear on what you do, and if he wants to know more, he can talk to you and ask specific questions. Typically, most won't, however, because they want to talk about themselves.

Firstly, I love this approach because you're answering people's questions. Some good networkers I know and respect teach to deflect the question and go right back to the person, but I've never liked that because you're dishonoring the question. It's almost like you're ignoring the question. Secondly, I love this approach because you quickly go back to the game, which is listening and asking them questions. This is important because people walk away and think *Man, that guy is a great conversationalist,* and you know you barcly said a word.

How do you enter a room and own it without saying a word? You prepare by creating space with yourself. You allow yourself to step into your own greatness with complete confidence because you're a Humble Alpha. You have zero expectations or cookie-cutter solutions in mind. You go in there and meet whoever you meet and determine you're going to elevate, elevate, elevate.

You'll add value and solve problems as they arise, but you're listening intently and asking questions. When you own that, and you know who you are, you just walk in. I walk in, stand in the middle of the door, and survey the whole operation. People may look and wonder, *Who is this guy?* You go to every single person if you can. If it's too many, you go to groups of people and introduce yourself. You might mention you hope to speak to them later when you head to the bar, or as you mingle around the buffet.

Meet each group of people, and if you hear or see something that impresses you—elevate!

Before I left for the army, my late grandfather Stanley Kuhn (bless his soul) told me not to be like everyone else. He told me to be the person who elevates. That's where the idea of elevating people comes from. Grandfather told me I could go out that very moment and stand in the middle of the sidewalk, and someone would have no problem pushing me out of the way while saying, *"Get out of the way, asshole."* However, if I stood on the side of the sidewalk, no one would come up to me and say, *"Hey, you look pretty cool."* No one would say anything to you unless you were in distress or in the way. He was right; not many people look around or give spontaneous compliments. He told me to be the person who compliments and makes people feel good; that if I saw something that impressed me, whether it was a man, woman, boy, or girl to call it out—always. I live by that, however, at the time, I was like, *"Thanks grandpa, can I have the keys to the car?"*

I'll see a guy in a bar and say, *"Dude, I don't know what you're doing here, but you can't be single. You're too good looking!"* I say it with zero expectations; I just want to compliment him because the guy looks good and takes care of himself. He might look at me and think: *What does this guy want?* He might think I want something, but there's no angle, so he ends up saying, *"Wow, thanks, man."* You can do the same thing with women, and it's a fantastic feeling to be a man who can do that, without making her feel like you're trying to pick her up.

Now when you elevate or give a compliment to a woman, don't say, *"You have beautiful eyes, or I love your body."* No, you might say, *"Wow, I love your glasses."* You're genuine, and if you don't see anything that impresses you, you don't say anything besides "Hi," and introduce yourself. You have to be genuine, or you come across like a cheeseball.

Appearance: The Path of Least Resistance

At networking events (and in our opinion, all of the time) you have to look presentable. You might wonder what that means. They say a dog is man's best friend, but for the men reading this, I say the ear and nose clipper is a man's best friend. Especially when you get up near my age. We've all been to a networking event where there's a guy with a squirrel hanging out everywhere. It's hard to talk to that guy and focus because you can't stop staring at his nose hairs.

Looking presentable is important. What are you wearing? Does it fit the occasion? Do you look like you give a damn? If you look like you give a damn, it gives the appearance that you give a damn about your business, and you're going to give a damn about me. A lot of people in today's world who love casual Fridays or run a business from home, don't get this.

If you walk up to me looking scruffy, you cannot give a damn. It's like going to court. If you go to court in a tank top and sweatpants, what's the judge going to say? *"Get out, come back when you've dressed more appropriately, and respect the court."* You're going into someone's court when you approach them, so you have to have respect for them. Show them that you give a damn because that's going to open up doors. You have to allow people to let you in; you can't force your way in. If someone walks up to me at a networking event wearing a cool hat, baggies, and no socks, it just doesn't fit well. I'm not going to judge that person at all, but they may be indicators about their ability to network and move forward with me.

When we talk about being well-dressed and keeping your appearance up, it's the path of least resistance. It's an external element of yourself. It's a reflection of who you are. People look at the external because that's what they can immediately see. It's the first thing they're going to see and make an assumption about when you're really trying to connect with them on an internal level. You want to get to a point where you're diving deeply into who they are and connecting with them on a personal, authentic, and genuine level. Whether you like it or not, caring about your appearance helps you get there more quickly.

You can't do that if you show up like Willie Lump-Lump. You insult their intelligence. Right now, there's a big trend of wearing t-shirts when you're speaking on stage. It's that *"I'm so cool I don't need to dress up,"* mentality. To me, that reflects on the respect that you have for the people who paid money to watch you speak or come to your event. I feel I owe it to people who attend my events to dress up and dress well. I want to physically demonstrate that I respect that they paid to hear and see me speak. I'm not going to be overdressed, but I am going to be intentional.

Take Gary Vaynerchuk, for instance, who wears a t-shirt, skinny jeans, and a beanie on stage. That might have been cool when he was 30, but he's 40-something now, and I personally think it's time for a change, but that's me. To his credit, he is changing his approach and has started to talk about empowering and loving people. A millennial might very well see this differently. If Gary V always wears t-shirts, it might seem a bit inauthentic to throw on a jacket. There's a very fine line between doing something that isn't authentically you, meeting people where they are, and demonstrating respect and gratitude. In this sense, Gary V may likely be spot on for his audience.

When you show up anywhere, you provide people with an experience in which they can be elevated. We're not saying to put on a three-piece suit with a vest and tie. I would put a jacket on over a t-shirt to the extent that the situation dictates.

A while ago, we did an event where we had two break-out sessions — one involved diving into the Humble Man and the other involved diving into the Authentic Alpha. I talked about how a Humble Man dresses.

I told them it's a good idea to own a white shirt, a blue jacket, a nice pair of jeans, a brown or black belt, or brown or black shoes at the very least. I talked about a pocket square, cufflinks, and the whole nine yards. I hit on the importance of having a wardrobe full of clothes you feel great in that you can wear to a wedding, a networking event, or anywhere you go. I even told them the secret of the white, short-sleeved v-neck undershirt. I wear it under my dress shirts and then if I'm going from a wedding to the bar, I take my nice shirt off, put my jacket back on, and I'm ready to go. Several guys in the group embraced it and went out and bought what I suggested.

One guy went to a restaurant with his wife in his Humble Alpha attire, and the people waiting to be seated stood up because they thought he was a bigwig since he wore a blue jacket over a white t-shirt. He said, *"Man, they asked me if I was the owner."* Can you imagine? Since he's started unleashing his Humble Alpha, he's getting more clients and referrals. They regularly invite him to lunch, and he's blown away because he used to show up in loafers, baggy jeans, and a t-shirt with his gut hanging out. No one ever invited him to lunch then.

People aren't going to invite you to lunch if you arrive like that, and what happens at lunch? You create a relationship, listen, and elevate them. That's how you get long-term clients and fans. It all happened because he started to give a damn. People no longer think he's just an IT guy they want to send into the back server room and close the door. Now, that's not saying anything bad about anyone's job. Please hear me out—I'm not saying that. I'm saying show respect for yourself and the people you're around by giving a damn about the external so you draw attention and can get to the internal with people.

Our Business Card Philosophy

I'm not a big fan of collecting business cards at networking events because it's me wanting something from people. If I have a conversation with someone and I have a genuine need for his or her service (or think I may in the future), that person is going to give it to me. I do have business cards that I rarely carry with me. I always forget them and nine times out of ten, I'm in a place where other Humble Alphas™ are hanging out and don't need them. I spoke in Vienna to about 500 people and handed out two business cards. One was to a journalist and the other to a Hungarian company that was interested in one of my services. My business card has my name and email on it; that's all it has.

You might think that's tricky, but it's not. If I'm in a place where I have to have business cards (because sometimes you have to have business cards), I don't want to give everyone my phone number. You don't want anyone and everyone calling you. If you do see someone that you want to talk to, you say, *"Hey, one second.."* and pull out your pen and write your number on the card. Then, that person's response is kind of like, *"Whoa, I'm getting his number."* Right there, I'm elevating that person and making him or her feel special because I'm writing my number on the card just for them. Not everyone gets my number.

This approach is how the Royals do it, by the way. I learned it from them. You'll remember the people who make an impression on you, and people will remember your name. If I hit it off with someone, I remember that person's name and connect with him or her on LinkedIn a couple of days later. I'll shoot him a quick message, say hi, and let him know it was great meeting him wherever we met. The people I didn't give a business card to will suddenly become an influx of LinkedIn contacts 2-3 days later.

At the end of the day, when you are living as a Humble Alpha and connect with someone deeply, you'll find a way to remain connected—business card or not.

Partnership Alignment

A key component to building momentum as a Humble Alpha is partnership alignment. We previously mentioned the Vetpreneur Tribe online community, and that's actually where Steven and I met. At the time, we weren't the leaders of it, but we were members who provided value. We messaged back-and-forth a bit in regards to attending a masculine awakening experience in Peru, but a couple of months went by and nothing happened. Then some of my friends in Panama went to Peru. They came back and told my wife and me about their trip. Immediately after that, my wife and I went and bought plane tickets for Peru. Since Steven and I had been messaging about Peru, we connected again and ended up meeting there later that year. We had an incredible experience, many epiphanies, and bonded to the extent that we started partnering up on things. Now, we're like brothers—probably even closer than real brothers.

Together, we've created a Humble Alpha experience in Peru that teaches men how to find their purpose and identity. It's very experiential based, as we use the sacred plant medicines of San Pedro and Ayahuasca. We use low doses, which literally get rid of blockages and open your mind to the possibilities you have. It's a practice used for millennia by the indiginous people, bringing about mental clarity and awakening that helps our attendees let go and explore who they are.

Past Performance, Present Values, and Future Vision

If you have a framework when you enter into partnerships, you'll save yourself millions. If you've had bad partners before, this is incredibly important.

If you haven't had a partner yet, this is an excellent framework to ensure you don't end up in a bad situation with a bad partner.

The way we met and partnered up was very intuitive because we have foundational partnership principles that we adhere to. When you break these principles down, they're: 1) past performance; 2) values you live by; and 3) vision for the future. These are three macro principles you can use to analyze a potential partner. They're pretty straightforward, but let's explore each one in detail.

When you look at past performance, you want to understand how quickly your potential partner accomplishes and executes tasks. The important thing here is that you're looking at just the performance, not the content of what he has performed or executed on. For me personally, I was in the special forces. I didn't have business experience, but I was a high-achiever and high-performer. I can apply many skills I learned in the special forces to high-level business. The main thing you're looking for is if this person has excelled, regardless of the area he's excelled in.

Past high-performance is an indicator that you'll probably do well together. You may have some learning curves and that's okay. If the partnership involves doing something that person has done his whole life and that's exactly what you're looking for, even better. Look for your potential partner's ability to bounce back from adversity; look for resiliency. Look at how he reacts when he runs into challenges or obstacles. Look at threads of detail. How he reacts to challenges can be indicators as to whether he's aligned for a potential partnership.

The second principle to look at is the present moment. Look at the values your potential partner lives by right now. Does he live his life honestly and transparently? Many people don't live by principles or if they do, they're loosely held. They might change when the wind blows. If a person lives his life intentionally, it's a good indicator that he's intentional in everything he does. How this person actually lives his life must be congruent with how he says he does.

You're looking for how your values align with a partner's; at least 80% of your values should line up. For example, we live our entire lives by H.I.T. (Honesty, Integrity & Transparency), which we'll discuss soon. Look at everything from how this person treats his family to whether he throws his garbage on the ground or in the trash can. Is his identity rooted in powerful principles and values? We're talking about the whole Life Enterprise.

When these seemingly intangible values are assessed and solidified during the formation of a partnership, many potential problems never happen. Follow this principle, and you dramatically reduce your risk of surprises down the road. No surprises means you're not worrying; you're only focused on crushing whatever you're doing. That focus is critical because it builds momentum quickly. When you're focused on your vision and mission, and nothing else is distracting you—including a lack of performance from a partner—you're in a very powerful position and primed for success.

The third principle is vision, and this one has to be flexible. You have to have a good idea of what your vision for the future looks like for you as a person and whatever you may co-create together. There's a fine line between having a concrete vision and also being open enough to allow for co-creation. When you create the space together and create the mastermind, you inevitably create an even bigger and better vision than what you had in mind as an individual. It's important that you go in having a vision for the future, but be open to how it'll transform. Just as important, the other person needs to be open-minded in the co-creation of the vision as well.

When it comes to vision, I've seen personal conflicts occur a lot because the vision was different between the individuals. One person may have 80% of the vision clarified and the other person may have 20% clarified, but together you make it whole. You have to be focused on the best ideas without clinging too firmly to any one in particular. You're always building upon ideas and fleshing things out. The bad ideas are going to get dropped, and what's going to be left (as long as you come in with a Humble Alpha persona) will be gold. Embodying the Humble Alpha persona is critical. Ego fans the flame of many conflicts.

Another important thing to remember is that the level of partnership dictates the intensity of how important these principles are in the selection of a partner. These principles always matter, but you can keep in mind the level that the partnership impacts your business. We're in a completely merged partnership so the alignment of each criterion is crucial. If I'm doing a joint venture with someone who provides a service to compliment my products, my business won't be drastically impacted if something goes awry because we're not intertwined. There's a varying degree of that, but we like working with really good people who are well-aligned.

When we first met, one of us had a coaching travel business where he'd take people into the mountains to break through, and the other had an offline consulting business. We both traveled, and that was about the only thing we had in common except our mindset and values. When we partnered, it took us about a year to flesh out our business and program, but it's centered around our values and vision, and we each bring very relevant skills from our pasts that apply.

It's important to find people who mirror who you are and align in the areas of their past performance, present, and future vision. How your partnership plays out might look very different. You might meet once a week, or you might speak on the phone a couple of times a month. Look at Steve Jobs and Steve Wozniak. They were partners, but you hardly saw them together. They did their own things and had their own opinions. They weren't hugging it out all of the time, but they had one vision together and made it happen.

A Co-Creator Not a Crutch

Another very important thing to note about selecting partners is that the person you choose shouldn't be a crutch for you. A lot of people who take on partners actually do so because they don't feel like they can run their business by themselves. They get a partner to help them. Your partner should be powerful in his realm, and you should be absolutely powerful in your realm. You shouldn't have to look over the other's shoulder, because you know what he's doing and he knows what you're doing. When the partner comes in, your focus should be on growth.

Strategic Alliances and Joint Ventures

Earlier in the book, I talked about how I partnered with Oliva Newton John on a supplement company. That was from the perspective of an individual fulfilling and acting on his own purpose and drive. From this point of view, we're talking about the actual organization and the company's desire to expand. I knew how to expand, so basically, I was aligned individually with fulfilling my purpose, and the company was aligned with fulfilling their purpose. It was co-creation, which is where the alignment piece is really critical. Previously, you saw it on an individual level, but here we're going to discuss it from an organizational standpoint.

Olivia's company is probably one of the most magical companies I've worked with because the alignment was so clear. It was incredible. After I met her and learned about the Amazon Herb Company, I reached out to find out how we could work together. I wanted to know how to bring the company to Europe because they weren't there. They sent a guy named Luke to talk to me, and we became inseparable. He moved to Budapest, and within six months, we'd brought Amazon Herb to six countries. It exploded because I was so aligned with them. They sent me all over Europe just to give my speech about why I chose them. I was a walking testimonial. It almost made me the face of the company in Europe because everyone knew who I was. Everywhere I went, I lived my credo. I was so thrilled with the results I got, other people—even doctors—were impressed.

People bought the herbs like crazy. I earned commission and provision (as they called it), so I got a little bit of this and a little bit of that. I would have never done that in another company. I would have had this, *"Pay me in advance, and we're good to go"* mentality. Money didn't matter because I was fulfilling my purpose and my values were aligned with the company. It just happened, and it became like a joint venture.

We all truly believed we were involved in something bigger than ourselves, which is why the venture worked so well. We contributed to the world and gave back. Giving the Amazon tribe back land that they legally should have owned is one of the most significant accomplishments.

Think about your life purpose and how your business is an extension or an amplifier of it. How powerful is it to create a business that's fully aligned with who you are and to partner with people who are truly aligned with you and your business? Your power and reach are amplified because you gain momentum by partnering. You create fulfillment in your life, in your partner's life, within your company, and in your customer's lives.

Wielding Influence

I have a friend in Austria who always introduces me to his friends. Any time I meet them, I listen and elevate. He's proud to introduce me because he knows I'm going to make them feel great.

One time, he introduced me to his friend and his friend's business partner. A little while after that, the business partner called me up and said, *"Hey, you're American, and you sort of work with everyone, right? Do you have contacts?"* I told him I did and asked what he had. He supplied the army and police in a particular country with their weapons, and he wanted to sell to the American government. I let him know he had to manufacture in America to do that; he couldn't just sell to the American government. He asked if I could set it up. I didn't think I could, but then I met a guy on an Island retreat I attend each year called The Baby Bathwater Institute. We talked about who manufactures weapons in America, and he had a contact. Everything came together.

I invested in relational capital every step of the way, and then I brought these three people together. I was paid very handsomely for facilitating the deal. That's how you wield influence and make money by investing in relational capital. It happens all of the time.

People say you can't take money to bring deals together, and this is where you have to differentiate between a strategic alliance and a referral. If someone comes to me and asks if I know someone who does a good job painting houses, if I do, I'll give him the name of an individual or company. Of course, I'm not going to ask for money.

If someone comes to me and says he needs a contact and specific data that takes time and effort to gather, then he needs to pay. Do you see the difference? If you have a problem that needs to be solved and I'm tapping into my influence to get it done, of course, I need to be compensated. That's wielding influence. You're creating the sum of the parts, and that's far bigger than the parts themselves. On their own, those three individuals could not have pulled that off, but by doing the legwork of collecting data and connecting them, it happened.

Meeting of the Minds

One of the wealthiest men I've ever spent time with privately approached me during a retreat and said, *"Damn, you're a big guy. How can I help? We're going to do it for you."* This guy is worth over $100 million, and that's his attitude on an island where no one is wearing shirts or shoes. We sat down and became friends. He actually flew from India where he lives to visit me in the hospital when I had surgery. The guy is one of the most authentic people I know, and I have massive respect for him as a human.

Masterminds, retreats, get togethers, and such are the greatest force for good in business. They are incredible because they stir up insuppressible energy and momentum. You're connected with people that are aligned with you in many different areas, whether personal or business. Such occasions can be incredibly potent ways to grow and contribute. You have to go in with the mindset that you're going to give more than you receive, however. When everyone does that, it's an incredible experience, The Baby Bathwater Institute does just that.

Such a mastermind can take place anywhere from a private Island in Croatia to a virtual meeting space. It doesn't matter where it's located. What's important is that you bring in your Humble Alpha energy of always providing value and elevating others. You have to invest in relational capital. It's the perfect place—a very potent place—to meet the right people and make the right connections.

A mastermind and event are two very different things, and a lot of people mix these up. An event takes place when you go to a hotel, sit in row seating, and listen to people speak from the stage with the hopes of selling something at the end. That's not a mastermind; a mastermind is free-flow-ing. No one pitches or sells. Everyone is there to add value, and everyone pays.

There is absolutely a place for events (we host them) because people need instruction and guidance. A mastermind comes in when your busi-ness is more solidified and you need to break through. Masterminds are powerful but choose wisely. Don't get caught up in the hotel or Airbnb VIP villa gig, no matter where it is. That's a person renting a villa, filling it with people, and bringing in some catering. That's a great retreat, but it's not a mastermind.

If you can simply sign up and join a mastermind, or if there isn't an interview or vetting process, it's probably not an authentic mastermind. If it's cheap, it's also probably not a mastermind. In real masterminds, you have to pay to play and that's part of the screening process. I know people who joined high-end masterminds when they didn't have two nickels to rub together. The question isn't: Do you have the cash sitting around? It's: Are you prepared to invest?

Creating Such Occasions

When we run retreats in Peru, we follow a loose structure and itinerary so people don't wonder what they're doing. However, it's fluid so we can be flexible with what the moment calls for. We're creating space, living in the present to elevate each other, providing solutions, and creating value.

While we're in Peru, we assess every moment and what it calls for. Because we do that, epiphanies and conversations with deep, profound meaning that change the trajectory of people's lives happen almost every hour. This goes on for eight to ten days, and because of its very nature, everyone comes away with incredible insights and clarity around who they are and what they're called to do. They leave ready to take the next steps towards greatness.

When you lead an event or mastermind, the first question to ask is: What problem am I solving? The next one is: Who am I inviting? Most peo-ple who run events and masterminds can't answer those questions directly. This goes for a one-on-one meeting or a convention, should you ever put one together. Recently, I was a speaker at a conference and I asked *"What is the solution you are providing? Why are people attending?"* They had no answer. I then said *"You have not sold out have you?"* And, of course, they didn't. You can sell tickets through booking big headliners, or you can sell tickets though providing tangible solutions for your specific demographic. Whatever you do, if you do it just to make money, the value will more than likely not be delivered. If you focus on delivering value and solutions, and elevate all those attending, you will need a larger arena next time you set it up. That is a promise.

During our last mastermind with a group of men, after we'd spent a few days in Peru, we utilized sacred herbs for mental clarity and had a guide drive us around to see sites. Then, we went to Machu Picchu.

We gelled as a unit. We'd worked together, been through traditional ceremonies, and we're all in a cohesive state. As we drove, all of a sudden, a car in front of us flipped over, hit a cliff, and fell back down on its roof. A guy was trapped inside, and by the time we got there, there were between 20-30 Peruvians freaking out. The guy inside was bleeding, and they didn't know what to do.

We looked at the guys and said, *"Guys, let's go."* Boom—we hopped off the bus, lined up along the car, and flipped it over on its side. We pulled the guy out and got back on the bus and left. We responded powerfully like it was no big deal. Why? How did this happen? Because we're so used to providing value and being solution-oriented that it's ingrained in everything we do.

We did it because it was the right thing to do; our character dictates that we do the right thing. Our group of men did it without even blinking. When we got back on the bus, we weren't like, *"Oh man, that was cool."* We didn't even talk about it, because that's how a Humble Alpha rolls.

Momentum isn't something you push out of yourself. It's something you create by being you. When you embrace your identity, your purpose crystallizes. Once you crystallize your purpose, it amplifies your identity. By investing in relational capital, creating space, and leading your life enterprise, you create momentum so you go faster and farther as a Humble Alpha. Everything is cumulative. The more you apply the lessons in this book, the more powerful you become. The more powerful you become, the less you need to show it, and the faster you move in the direction of your mission.

Before You Continue

As we wrap up this stage (and before you go through the action steps), take a moment and imagine what life will look like when every relationship is on fire. What does life look and feel like? How amazing does it feel to go to any event and crush it? How does it feel to know you'll always attract the right business partners and partnerships? Grab your bookmark, save this spot, and put this book down. Do this mental exercise and then continue to the action steps.

Action Steps

Congratulations on making it to the end of stage four! Before you take action on these steps, be sure you've completed all of the action steps for the previous stages. It's vital you do the previous work before taking action below, because they all build upon one another.

Break down the following action steps into bite-sized actions. The material in this stage applies to these action steps, as well as situations in previous stages. Take action, and focus on small incremental progress. Do the work, and let all the action steps in this book build on one another. You've got this.

Remember, action steps are things that are in your control, they are something you can do. They aren't outcomes, which are things outside of your immediate control. Here they are:

1. **Invest in Relational Capital** – Create space with every person you meet, and invest in each relationship fully.

2. **Networking** – You may attend events regularly, or you may have never attended one. If you go to a lot of events, continue to go to the events and implement the strategies in this stage. If you don't regularly go to events, challenge yourself to go to one of each below within the next 12 months. Be sure to practice the strategies and techniques in this stage.

   a. Events

   b. Masterminds

   c. Retreats

3. **Partnerships & Joint Ventures** – These are entirely dependent on you. You will decide when it's time to expand your company via partnerships. You will decide when you will participate in joint ventures. But when you do, fully embrace your Humble Alpha, and trust you know what to do.

As you're taking action on these specific steps, be sure to embed the "intangible" aspects of this stage. The intangibles are just as important as implementing the tangible action steps. Deadlines are less important for these action steps, but ensure you prioritize these steps nonetheless.

Bookmark this page to keep track of your next action step. You can also download this checklist, along with other worksheets, resources, and videos that help you dig more deeply into these exercises. These bonuses are free of charge and come along with this book. To get them, go to: HumbleAlpha-Book.com/bonus

Section Five

LEBENSQUALITÄTE

⟿

"What you leave behind is not what is engraved in stone monuments, but what is woven into the lives of others."

— Pericles

One cannot have Quality of Life, without being conscious of how he spends each moment. The energy and enthusiasm you bring to each moment will radiate light to all around you. The quality of the life you live will determine the quality of the legacy you leave behind.

Each cherished moment lived wholly and fully will leave more of a lasting effect than anything physical could. Money and resources can be acquired by any means, but your time and attention are the most prized gifts you can give to those you care about. Just knowing you lived and brought goodness to the world, can be life's greatest reward.

What Is Lebensqualitäte?

Lebensqualitäte is a German word that means Quality of Life. When you live an abundant Quality of Life, ease surrounds you, not because life is easy, but because you're operating from a place of confidence, strength, and security. For example: You may get contracts from clients around the world, even though you're not marketing. At this stage in your journey, your company is thriving, and you can sense the ambition, passion, and humility within your company culture. Every member of your team is in hot pursuit of unleashing his or her Humble Alpha, and unexpected opportunities present themselves around every bend. Everything is in alignment. When you embody the principles in this book and unleash your Humble Alpha, you'll be at ease with your wife, kids, and in your relationships. You'll live in the present moment and enjoy the fullness of each day.

A Day in the Life of a Humble Alpha

A Humble Alpha lives purposely. He's intentional about how he allocates his time and attention. His day is full of meaning because he sets it up that way.

I begin my day by meditating and journaling. Next, the most significant moment comes. My wife and I fill our cups with piping hot coffee and settle into our overstuffed sofa. The kids lay across our legs, and we use this carved out time to enjoy and appreciate one another. Every day, I recognize who they are as human beings and show gratitude for them. Then we take the children to school and my wife and I head to the gym to train together. I am so thrilled to be able to train with my wife; this is another special time of the day where we are 100% there for each other consciously. We sweat, push, pull, and laugh together. It is so fulfilling, I cannot even put it into words. After the gym, my wife and I head home for breakfast and some more together time. Then I head to my home office and begin my workday, which typically starts with client calls.

When I travel (which is not as much as it used to be, but still often enough), I ensure I have scheduled time to speak on video calls with her and the children. We also keep each other "interested" during my absence. That can be through loving text messages, pictures, or just a *"Hey, I am doing this and thinking of you."* I use the time away to dig deeply, feel what my life is all about, and how my wife is so incredibly important to me, and then I tell her. This keeps things fresh, new, and—dare I say—exciting! This keeps me on my A-Game wherever I am. She knows it and consciously deploys these tactics to keep me there. It's all done in love and contribution, and it is amazing.

Imagine laughing mid-day about a sexy text from your wife, or walking into a boardroom and walking out with a retainer when it takes most men months to get through the pyramid of gatekeepers. People wonder why we're so happy and what our secret is; this is it! What we've laid out for you is how we're able to live on purpose, love on purpose, and dominate in every sphere of life.

Lebensqualitäte doesn't happen by accident. You prepare for it through thousands of deliberate seconds every single day of your life. Is it time to start the clock in your life?

H.I.T.
(Honesty, Integrity, and Transparency)

To unpack this idea of a Quality of Life that exceeds your expectations and feeds your soul, let's dig into two key principles along with some supporting strategies. The first principle is H.I.T.(honesty, integrity, and transparency). H.I.T. leads to trust, and trust leads to manifesting what you want in life.

We've all had experiences in life when we've shown up, and great things happened. We tend to look at the results of our showing up (or what happened) and not how we did it in the first place to get those results. We don't make a record, so over time, we wonder how we won, came out unscathed, improved a situation, or overcame a tremendous obstacle. That's when we start asking questions.

At the end of my first marriage, I lost my job, marriage, money—everything— within a week. I sat there and didn't know what to do. I had a shoebox full of scraps of paper with thoughts on them I'd written down years earlier. I'd scribble thoughts down when I worked in bars and it was slow, or nothing was going on. I'd write my thoughts about my time in the Gulf War. In Iraq, I did the same thing and wrote down how I felt at certain moments. These were things like, *"Holy shit. I remember the time they asked for volunteers, and I didn't put my hand up until someone else did."* I wrote thoughts like that.

Some friends ruffled through my shoebox, read a few slips of paper, and said, *"Hey, you need to write a book."* So I did.

I lived in Germany at the time and took the notes, made them into a four-page synopsis, and sent it to publishers. One publisher wanted to look at it and wrote an article in the newspaper. It came out in 2003—the day the current Iraq War began. I hadn't finished writing or editing the book, and it was already a bestseller. Everyone pre-ordered it, and I made a TV appearance immediately. I was on TV the day after the war started. Twenty to twenty-five million people watched the American Ambassador to Germany, the British Ambassador to Germany, and all kinds of famous people speak, and everyone looked at me because I was the only German-speaking American combat veteran at the table.

I went through the questions they'd prepared for me, and then someone asked me if I supported the war. I never thought of the war that way. I never thought of that question, because I'm an American, patriot, and veteran. Of course, I support the war, right? When I thought about the ideology behind it, however, I didn't support the war because of the way we went about it. I'm a patriot; I love my country, but I didn't support what it was doing. For a few milliseconds, I didn't know how to answer that question transparently because my mind raced with what the Americans wanted to hear and what the Germans wanted to hear. Then, I thought, *"Screw it; stay true to your identity."* My response poured out of me, and I spoke powerfully about how I support my fellow soldiers and my government, but that I believed the war was wrong.

I got nailed. The Germans loved me. Of course, the axis of evil, right? But I had death threats from people who called me at two o'clock in the morning to say things like, *"I know where you live."* It was terrible, but I had zero fear because that's who I was.

Honesty and transparency look like that, and they're significant character values for the Humble Alpha, especially in moments when it's the most difficult to be honest and transparent. The gentleman on TV told me that it took a lot of integrity to say what I did in front of that many people, and it did.

The concept of H.I.T. comes from this, but I didn't turn it into an acronym until later. As a self-employed General Manager in the corporate world—when I ran between nine countries training team members—it emerged. People started calling me the HIT Man, and it stemmed from that nickname. Let's break each component down.

Honesty

Honesty is the keystone of the principles. Honesty begins internally and then moves its way outward into the external world. Honesty means to be true to who you are and how you live.

To begin the process of being honest with ourselves, we need to take responsibility. That means we aren't blaming others for where we are in life. They didn't "do" anything to us. We must understand that we always have a choice in life. It is our decisions in life that have brought us to this moment in time. Circumstances in the past cannot—and will not—dictate our future, unless we allow it to. This responsibility needs to be taken 100% without any conditions or caveats.

Integrity

Integrity is the byproduct of living by honesty and transparency. Integrity becomes your reputation. When you live with integrity, your desires and goals will seem to magnetize to you out of nowhere. Integrity is that magical glue that attracts what you desire.

Continuing to live a life of honesty and transparency will keep your integrity intact. Integrity is always the byproduct of acting in accordance with honesty and transparency. The quote *"Doing the right thing, even if no one is looking"* sums it up nicely. If you lie, your integrity is compromised. If you stretch the truth, your integrity is compromised. If you leave out key parts of the truth, your integrity is compromised. You get the idea.

That's why when you observe others that compromise their integrity for small things, you won't be surprised if they compromise their integrity for big things as well. Once integrity is compromised in one area of life, it can be compromised all around. This means integrity can't be compartmentalized; it's all-encompassing.

Transparency

Communicating your honesty is what transparency is all about. It's saying and acting in accordance with who you really are. That's why being honest with yourself comes first. You need to know who you truly are before you can communicate your true self to others. What others see of you is what they get. Being "transparent" with someone who you are not, actually isn't being transparent.

Transparency is being able to take your internal beliefs, values, and vision into the outer world. You do this by translating these into actionable behaviors. If you believe family comes first, how do you act on that belief? If you value your friendships, what does that look like in the real world?

Your actions are the visible, tangible expression of yourself. It's what people see, therefore, you should act with intention. Intentional action, in alignment with your values and beliefs, will ensure you are communicating your honesty. Being intentional does require effort in the beginning, but becomes second nature with practice. By being intentional, you slowly become more intuitive. You'll intuitively be more honest and unveil your best self over time.

Communication is knowing how to deliver the truth to the person or audience you are communicating with. To best do that, you need to see the world and the message you are sharing from their perspective first. You are always being honest, but by approaching the delivery of the message from their perspective, you can resonate with them more effectively and more authentically.

For example, let's take the topic of the work you do. You explain your work to your nephew differently from how you would explain it to someone else in the same industry as you. Right? You are tailoring the message to the recipient. You want to effectively get across what you do so you quickly step into their shoes and understand how best they would likely receive the message. Then you deliver it. You are always being honest, yet you are ensuring you provide a relevant contribution to the situation.

Transparency is a two-way street. You can't expect to give transparency and not receive it. People can and should share their honest opinion of things, so you should expect them to act in such a way. Because you know yourself well, any constructive feedback will be taken well and used to make yourself better.

Transparency means being open about what you think, feel, and experience. You don't hold back because you're afraid, but at the same time, you're not someone who rattles off everything that comes to mind because you have to "make your truth known."

A Deeper Look at H.I.T.

Honesty is stepping out and saying who you are—good, bad, judgment, or no judgment. When you're honest like that, no one can have anything on you. It doesn't matter what people say about you. If someone talks about you, it doesn't affect you because it doesn't change who you are. You're your most authentic self, and you're not holding back.

Honesty applies to your identity and purpose, and you must bring honesty into this process. When you ask yourself questions about why you do what you do and look at how you define your identity and interact with the world, be critically honest with yourself because this is the core of who you are. If you don't, you lie to yourself. People don't want to help you if you're inauthentic. When you're authentic, people naturally want to help you with what you're doing. Honesty also applies to how you assess and look at your company.

Sometimes it's hard to take an honest assessment of where your company is and where you need to improve. It's hard to get honest and admit that your communication isn't excellent or that you haven't embedded Quality of Life in your company culture. Take a hard look at your organization and bring honesty into the process.

When it comes to networking, honesty is very important, too. When you speak with someone, invest in relational capital, and build relationships, you can't build authentic relationships or lasting connections if you're not honest. It's all interconnected.

We can't be dishonest and think we're honest because honesty begins internally and then moves its way outward. Honesty is vital to growth. Without honesty, you don't grow.

When we're dishonest, we put blinders on, and we only see what we want to see. Honesty is not only expressing what you say but what you demonstrate with your actions. This is why you need precise language; it's why you hear us talk very precisely. When you're honest with yourself, you shine a light on the good and bad stuff in your life, and you can reach your highest level when you bring the bad elements out of the shadows and deal with it.

Honesty equals reliability because people know you as honest, and people stand behind your honesty. Some people lie so much, they get lies and truth confused. It's because we'll tell small, white lies to avoid suffering, shame, change, embarrassment, or conflict. H.I.T. solves this by getting to the core of the shame, suffering, or embarrassment challenge.

We also tell fibs or lies to get what we want. H.I.T. solves this by allowing you to get what you want without the risk of a lie backfiring on your efforts. Sometimes we want others to think highly of us or we protect other people's feelings, so we don't tell the truth. A Humble Alpha can't do that.

We cover H.I.T. at the very end of the five stages of unleashing your Humble Alpha because it takes aspects from every corner of the journey to get here. At this stage in your journey, you organically attract others who live by H.I.T. It results in authentic connection, significance, and genuine happiness.

With H.I.T., you show up fully present for whatever comes. In today's world, you see people who follow trends because they want to be someone else or have what someone else has. They're not living their true lives because they don't know how to do so. They don't know who they are. Through this Humble Alpha journey, we dig through all the layers so you can live honestly and transparently with integrity. Typically, people who follow trends don't know what they like or what they're worth.

By being honest with another person, he can successfully make a change in his life because you told him the truth. When you're honest, you get to the core issue and solve it permanently. You also remove stress, anxiety, and shame, which are the symptoms of a root issue.

The thing about lying is when you're used to lying, you justify it, and then suddenly it becomes your 'truth'. You actually believe your lies. In business, this happens a lot. You might like a guy and not want to fire him, so you convince yourself he's not doing that bad. You're lying to yourself. In the corporate world, you see this culture where they've created little white lies, and even come up with different words for them. The other day, I heard someone say, *"We're not lying; we're assessing."* I don't even know what that means.

Puffery is the "legally allowed" exaggeration of marketing claims. Copywriting is key in marketing to create an emotional attachment that moves people to buy, but people can sense when you're trying to pull the wool over their eyes. Honesty is always better. There's even a copywriting approach called the "Candor Lead," that starts a sales letter by being forthright and transparent about all of your flaws, lack of experience, and limitations. People think that if they lack authority or expertise, they have to puff things up, but in an age of over-hyped promises, transparency lowers people's defences and makes everything else you say more believable.

You may win the short term battle with puffery, but you won't win prospects by deceiving them, and eventually, they'll discover what you're up to. What good does that do, especially at the beginning of your relationship?

When Is it Okay to Lie?

By its very nature, this is a question we get all the time. If I'm being honest all the time, is it ever okay to lie? It's never okay to lie. You don't lie. You always have to tell the truth. However, here's the deal. When it comes to transparency, you shouldn't tell your competitors everything, right? You must be honest and transparent to the degree that the situation dictates that each of you have a win-win. Remember, you're elevating others and leaving them in a better place than they were before. You don't need to tell people everything that isn't pertinent to the situation. Some people say it's withholding information, but it's not. If you're assessing the situation and providing information so that everyone has a win-win, you're not lying. You don't have to show your revenue or reveal your biggest marketing secrets; you do what the situation dictates from your place as a Humble Alpha .

A win-win situation prevents harm and elevates everyone. We lie to avoid harming others or to protect ourselves, but we don't need to. People think lying is a good strategy to protect someone's feelings, but you want to get to the core of the problem and solve it to get what you want. Be straightforward. I don't have a problem being open about challenges or issues I'm having. If you did something, be the first to admit it and own your mistake. You say, *"Oh wow, I messed up. Let's fix this; how can I do that?"*

One of my biggest complaints about politicians is that there's such a vested interest in never admitting a mistake; no one ever owns up to one. Transparency is about communicating honestly.

When you operate as a Humble Alpha and are honest with other people, it doesn't have a sort of intangible energy that makes the person feel like you're judging him. You're always honest from a place of elevation because you genuinely want people to step into their greatness.

We make the mistake of assuming that honesty is harsh; that you're telling someone how it is. A Humble Alpha always comes from a place of elevation, so the interaction is as different as night is from day. Honesty is so important because that's where we pull everything from. Without a core honesty about who you are or what you do, you won't have as much power or impact.

In the special forces, we had after-action debriefs where everything was laid on the table. We discussed what was supposed to happen, what really did happen, and how we could improve. When you discuss how to improve, you must bring the Humble Alpha energy and not blame anyone. When you get a whole bunch of people together trying to unpack a situation, sometimes it doesn't work out exactly how you thought it was going to. In this context, by taking an honest assessment and bringing in the facts, you can prevent a life or death situation.

The higher the level of transparency and honesty you demonstrate, the quicker trust is built, which means more people are more apt to help you in your efforts. Others also connect to you more organically when you're honest and transparent.

How to Live By H.I.T.

Living an honest life is about calibrating yourself back into alignment. You must accept reality as it is presented to you. Only then are you able to shape reality at will. By not fully understanding reality, you will not be able to change it. You must make each decision—moment by moment—honestly.

You may need reminders to keep yourself honest. Triggers, affirmations, reminders, and questions are some ways to do this. Figure out the best way that reminds you to always live in honesty.

Living by H.I.T. can be difficult in the beginning, so here's an easy way to get started. Make small intentional promises to yourself, then keep them. How often do you hear yourself saying to others, *"Yes! Let's hang out sometime soon!"* Then nothing ever happens. You forget, they forget; until you run into them serendipitously again. Instead of saying things you really don't mean, make a promise to yourself that you will follow up on your word. These small promises start small, but then you start to notice bigger promises that you've been breaking to yourself. This sounds simple, and it is, but it's so powerful.

Holding yourself responsible for keeping your word, even for the small things, will create a great sense of deserved pride. A lack of accountability will lead to keeping your word less frequently. You are making a commitment to yourself—the most important commitment you can make in your life.

Throughout the day, invite your most honest self to join you. You can do this by reminders or asking yourself a simple question, "Am I being honest right now"? This question isn't a judgment, but rather an objective question to ensure you are being 100% honest with yourself. After you answer, act according to your best, honest self.

Living by H.I.T. allows your best self to reveal itself the majority of the time. Sometimes you may need a reminder as to what to do next or how to take action. You want to do this in accordance with your best self. A great question to ask yourself often is: "what would my best self do right now?" After asking, then answer it honestly and take action.

These questions can be thought of as checking your compass from time to time. The majority of your journey will be enjoyed in the present moment. From time to time, you need to check your compass to make sure you're moving in the right direction towards your vision. These questions are your compass checks ensuring you are heading true north.

Constantly living by H.I.T. means that you will be wrong eventually. If you refuse to "be wrong", then you really aren't living by H.I.T. When you come across an idea that many people disagree with, you may want to ask yourself a question. It also may be something that several people who care about you approach you about. Ask yourself this question: Am I willing to risk being wrong? If you aren't willing to be wrong, then you really don't want to know the truth. That means you care more about being right than knowing the truth. Be willing to be wrong when you are. Be honest and admit mistakes.

This willingness to change indicates you can let go of false beliefs and grow. Change is happening all the time; it's all there is, actually. By adapting to new or updated information, you can adapt to always becoming your best self and being able to provide more value to the world.

Knowing how to say "no" is an important part of living by H.I.T. This means that you know yourself well enough that if something doesn't resonate or isn't in alignment with you, then you won't do it. It doesn't matter if you're tempted by reward or money, you know it won't fulfill you. So you don't do it.

Living by H.I.T., you may notice yourself not "fitting" in with the crowd. This is neither good or bad, it's just you understanding yourself better and living authentically. You may actually notice the crowd moving toward you. Because you have a sense of purpose and know exactly who you are, people will gravitate toward you. The right people and the right crowd will be drawn to you as you are also drawn to them.

It's Easier to Live Life Honestly

The world is full of fakers, and it takes a lot of effort and energy to be someone you're not day-in-and-day-out. H.I.T. makes it easier to live your life; you don't have to try to remember what you said, to whom you told it, and when. You also automatically shield yourself from distrustful people because they know you're going to call them out.

Remember, we all make mistakes, and it's better for you to be transparent about those mistakes than for someone else to reveal them. As you're transparent, others are inspired to be more transparent, and soon the world is a more transparent place.

The internet and advancing technology are making the world more transparent. It's better to be ahead of the curve and live by H.I.T. The world values honesty much more than it used to, and it's becoming a more honest place. In politics, you see people bringing the truth to light through the news, their own media and blog posts, and through protests.

Certainty

If we boil everything down in this entire book, the result of unleashing your Humble Alpha can be summed up in two things: Quality of Life and certainty. Your Quality of Life spans every sphere of your life: your relationships, health, business—everything.

When you're certain, you know something is going to happen. The Humble Alpha journey creates certainty in your life. Our clients and students emerge and let go. They don't worry about how they'll get to where they want to go, because they're certain they'll get there. Most people micromanage the journey in hopes of getting to the destination. We create the life we want to live and the landscape we want to play on, and then through habit stacking and all of these principles, we allow the path to unfold knowing that when we live like this every day, we'll get to our destination. Certainty is your engine.

The beautiful house I live in now, we manifested in three months through certainty. We signed the purchase agreement without the money. I didn't even worry about it because I knew the money was coming because I'd seen it already happen.

Back in 1998, when I lived in Berlin, I heard on the radio that a popular American band was coming to the city and the bodyguard was staying in London because he'd hurt himself on stage. Anyone else who heard that wouldn't pay attention. I thought, *Oh wow, I've always wanted to work for this guy,* and I was certain I could make it happen, so I walked right into the hotel where the band was staying and greeted the staff by name.

I could walk into the hotel while this famous band was there because I elevated the gastronomic community in Berlin by having a special night every week for restaurant and bar owners to enjoy half-price cocktails. In the end, anyone who worked in a bar, restaurant, or hotel could come to my place and drink half-price all day long.

After I walked into the hotel and greeted everyone, I went to the lobby area in the back and waited for this band to come down. I walked up to the musician, and I said, *"Hey, Mick Jagger. I'm your new bodyguard."*

He said, *"What? Who sent you? What do you mean?"*

I said, *"I sent me. Your bodyguard is staying in London, because he hurt himself. I'm certified. I speak German. I know the city like the back of my hand, and I'm a war veteran who knows how to protect you."*

He said, *"Talk to CJ,"* who was his security chief. CJ told me he had one question for me, and if I answered it, I had the job.

He asked, *"Do you know where to get the best German sausage?"*

"I sure do," I replied.

He goes, *"You got the job. How does $400 a day sound?"*

It took less than a minute to get a temporary dream job and hang out with Mick Jagger for three weeks. If you ever want to talk to someone who's famous or you want to get someone's attention and you're in a crowd, use that person's entire name—first and last. That's the key to getting their attention because it's disruptive. No one walks around saying hi to you using your first and last name. At the time, I didn't know this was my Humble Alpha in action, but it was. My Humble Alpha was certain I could make it happen, and I did.

Another time, I was at the gym talking with great certainty to a game warden about how to get a license to go wild boar hunting and the topic drifted into the Peru experience Lane and I hold each year. He asked me what I do for a living. I told him and didn't think anything of it. The whole time, there was someone standing in my peripheral view who I didn't know was listening to me. Three days later, he came up to me and said, *"Hey, I want to come to Peru."* I didn't know who he was, but he saw me talking to the warden and said he'd never heard anyone speak with such certainty and directly. He came to Peru, and now he's one of our best friends.

Wherever you are, consistently amplify your purpose and identity. Once you start, it becomes more and more effortless. Your newly created habits, secure identity, and clear purpose create certainty in how you think, speak, and act. Certainty is the end product of this experience. When you walk down the street, and you're certain about who you are and what your purpose is, everyone knows there's something different about you. Why? Because you're a freaking Humble Alpha.

Enjoying the Present

A well-known quote, by Annie Dillard, sums this principle up. It says, *"How we spend our days is, of course, how we spend our lives."* Moments make up your day. Enjoying the present moment is the definition of Quality of Life.

Whether you're coaching your favorite client, on a hike with your family, or traveling on an airplane to a high-level mastermind, you should equally enjoy and appreciate every moment. I'm sure by now you think that all sounds great, but what happens when things get tough? It's challenging to enjoy a terrible moment, but we've gotten to a place in our lives where we embrace every challenge that comes our way. We appreciate obstacles and hardships because they're catalysts for growth. Absorb everything you can from that terrible moment, tuck those lessons into your toolbox, and trudge through until you come out smiling on the other end.

If stress and frustration hog the moments in your day, leaving very little for passion, fun, and happiness, get rid of them. If you want to change tomorrow, you need to do it now, at this moment. You can't change certain things, but you can change how you respond to them. If you hate rain and it's raining right now, you can't do anything about that. Why choose to fill that moment in time with hate?

We all know not to walk down a dark alley. Even if we kick ass and take names, it still invites trouble. You have to start seeing your negative emotions and thought patterns as dark alleys. Don't go down the negative street. Do you know who lives there? Negative Nelly. And you sure as heck don't want to be married to her, or even keep company with her, for that matter. At some point in life, however, you will go down dark alleys no matter how much you try to avoid them, but here's the secret: That Humble Alpha nuclear reactor inside of you will light the path, even in the darkest of times.

If you're pursuing happiness, you'll chase it endlessly. You can't pursue happiness. Like a flame, you fan it, and it sparks from within. You stir it up until it rises to the surface. We talk about appreciation and gratitude. Those two principles are the tinder (no—not the swipe-right Tinder) that'll cause your fire to combust. Whether you're enjoying a cup of coffee with your family or a light traffic day on your commute, pause and appreciate that moment. When you tap into that sphere of gratitude, the same amount of appreciation you have for that frothy cup of coffee is the same amount of satisfaction you have for a million-dollar deal. You demonstrate equal energy and equal certainty.

Living in the present moment looks like hundreds of these moments stacked one on top of the other; it's how you ignite happiness. You have to embed these practices of gratitude and appreciation into your habits and routines.

Scheduled QOL and Recharge

Scheduled QOL stands for scheduled Quality of Life. This builds on what we discussed earlier with habit stacking and creating routines. You bring intention to your Quality of Life by outlining it and scheduling time to recharge. One of the formulas we subscribe to is growth = stress + rest. When we work out, we stress our muscles. We're breaking them down to a certain extent, so they can rebuild stronger. When we rest, those muscles rebuild. The same applies to our lives; we also need rest periods. When you lift weights to build muscle, the ratio of stress to rest for that building process is very unbalanced. The stress on your muscles is a small percentage of the entire process of getting stronger. A significant amount of the building occurs while you're at rest. This sets up the conditions for growth.

This same principle applies to everything that you're doing in life. By intentionally carving out time for rest, you ensure growth happens. How many times have you missed sleep due to stress from your business, relationships, or finances? Doesn't progress and momentum stall out or plateau when you have more stress than rest?

Flow Research Collective is a peak-performance research and training organization and a world-leading voice on flow science. A friend of ours there taught us a concept known as hedonic calendaring. Hedonic calendaring looks like this: Every day you have specific activities dedicated to rest, recharge, and Quality of Life. Every week you have a full day dedicated to those activities. Then, every month you have a whole weekend dedicated to those activities. Next, every quarter you participate in a more significant moment of rest, recharge, and Quality of Life, however that may look for you. The general idea is that you schedule rest with intention and focus on it because it's an essential aspect of your life.

This is exactly why we have our retreat in Peru and why we work with sacred plant medicine. I've worked with sacred plant medicine for 15 years now. It's very grounding and relaxing. It's typically used by indigenous tribes to break through this world and find one's real purpose and identity. Our minds are programmed with limitations, false ideas, and scarcity. The use of the plant is very appealing because all of that fades away.

We stay in a compound in the middle of the Incan ruins, so we're fully immersed in the culture. We don't drive for hours to see sites. We can easily hire a guide for a nearby visit. We are also a minute's walk from the Temple of the Moon; another minute, and we're at the Temple of the Frog. The throne of the Incan King and marriage thrones are right there. If you believe in energy (which everyone should), then you know this energy is ever present.

We use musical instruments that vibrate deep into every cell in your body. Peru is our scheduled yearly time to recharge, and we intentionally build the experience around those concepts. If this is something that interests you, we'd love to invite you. For more information about our Humble Alpha Peru Retreat, visit HumbleAlphaBook.com/peru.

Whether it's going on a retreat, meditating, getting outdoors, going to the gym, or getting massages, you must rest and recharge. We all know the people who—and you may be one of them—book two weeks out of the entire year to rest, relax, and recharge. You're on vacation, doing this, and seeing that, but the whole time you're still unwinding from a jam-packed year and life. Once you get home, you still feel like you didn't fully relax. You may do that, and it's okay because we're providing you with a concept for how you can rest more intentionally and integrate it into your daily life.

You have to own this aspect of your life because we calibrate rest in consistent micro increments every single day, week, month, and quarter. As you hike, meditate, bike, or journal, you shed stress; it's like you're shaking its crumbs off of your life each day, so it never builds up. This is how you keep your stress low. And what else do these activities do? They fulfill you and amplify your happiness, too, which leads to better relationships, unrestrained creativity, higher performance, and bottomless innovation.

By scheduling rest and Quality of Life, you create lebensqualitäte. You build your lifestyle one block at a time based on what you need to attract what you desire. Think about that saying, *"If you resist, it'll persist."* If you resist scheduling rest and Quality of Life, what unhealthy practices will persist?

When you make plans for rest, paint a picture of the future. Every year when we plan our retreat to Peru, we paint a very vivid picture of it. Planning and painting a vision of the future isn't just a thought in our minds; it's who we are and what we do. We plan big and small things because it leads to massive growth. It supports the amplification of our Humble Alpha. Stagnation leads to atrophy, and it's a real danger to every principle you embody. We always plan our rest, which leads to constant growth.

Date with Your Significant Other and Strength Trainer

If you don't have regular date nights with your significant other, book one in your calendar for every week right now. If you work out and do strength training haphazardly, put your gym sessions in your calendar right now. If you don't think about nutrition and whether or not you're eating enough to lose weight (it's counterintuitive, yes!), schedule your meal times in your calendar right now.

Don't let this go in one ear and out the other. These aren't meetings with external people or activities; these are meetings with yourself. The most important meeting all day is the one you have with yourself. Internalize this; and schedule.

Scheduling puts you in your optimal position, and if you're not grounded, how will you ever provide for anyone around you to your maximum ability? As the CEO of your life enterprise, you owe it to your stakeholders to operate at your highest level at all times. The only way to do that is to take yourself seriously and make yourself a priority. You're not being selfish or running hard 24/7. It means you're intentional with your physical, mental, spiritual, and emotional states at all times, even when you rest.

I scuba dive and when you go on vacation and do a lot of diving, you have to rest. If you don't, you get the bends, which is decompression sickness. You're forced to rest on the beach then dive; rest on the beach then dive. On a particular vacation, we dived one day and relaxed the next day for nine days straight. It's my favorite trip I've ever taken, and now I know why. Diving every single day is exhausting and risky. When you create a sort of void and then step back in, you experience both the joy of rest and activity to their fullest measure.

Full Integration of Business and Life

Richard Branson is always skydiving, windsurfing, or hanging out on his private island. In his business and personal life, he does a multitude of exciting things. He has a variety of companies, and you see the handprint of his identity on each one. He has fully integrated his business and life.

There's no difference between your life enterprise and your business. Everything is interconnected, but that doesn't mean you let business bleed into your home life and your home life bleed into your business. We're always Humble Alphas™; we're not two different people, but we know what we need to focus on and when, even though everything is connected. When things are going well at home, they naturally go better in business, but you can't let your home life be an excuse for your business performance. The "happy wife, happy life" saying is so popular because it has this connotation that when you're happy at home, you're happy at work. Your happy life isn't dependent on a happy wife. It helps, yes! But, you're a freaking Humble Alpha.

When I met my wife, I told her that I travel all of the time and I love to do it. She told me as long as I was happy, she was happy. She loved me and supported me, and that was fine. If someone else is responsible for your happiness, you have an expectation of them. Expectations guarantee a disaster because, at some point, someone won't meet your expectations. We're all human, and we all make mistakes.

Being happy and learning to love yourself isn't always a straightforward journey; that's why we have the Humble Alpha Leadership Program. A long time ago, I went to an Austrian monastery for a few months and meditated, chanted, and prayed with the Benedictine monks to find out how I could love myself. I invested in myself to get there. I didn't pay bills or tell anyone except my parents where I was going. I simply disappeared. As a six-foot-four-inch, 280-pound man, that's saying something. It looked pretty funny. I'd been a director of a big European company, and there I was crushed because I couldn't find love. Once I found it within myself, all my desires for a woman completely disappeared because I was happy being with myself.

Shortly after my stay in the monastery, I had a contract offer in Budapest. There I sat on the steps of St. Stephen's cathedral—the second largest cathedral in Europe— in the middle of the day and meditated in front of everyone. That's how solid I was; how incredible I felt with myself. I could shut out 6,000 people taking pictures. I was utterly alone—and you're okay with being utterly alone when you're a Humble Alpha—and attracted my wife, the perfect woman. It was pure alignment. I saw her and knew in a minute that she was my wife. Ten years later, she's still the perfect woman, and every day with her is a blessing.

When we talk about full integration of life and business and we share these things, remember they aren't theory. We've applied this to our own lives; it's how we live. You fully integrate the Humble Alpha. Think about integration this way: If you conduct a meeting at work and your wife is watching, would she be disappointed or think to herself, *Oh yeah, that's him!* The same goes for at home. If you're at home having dinner with your wife and your team members are watching, would they be disappointed or think, *Wow, he's great with everyone!* That's how you act in your business and life.

We demonstrate this to our clients through what we call our "Coaching by Osmosis" service. When a client wants high-performance mindset coaching or a person wants some fitness coaching, I have them come over to my house for a week in Hungary. Now, at my home, we speak German, Hungarian, and English and when clients come, they often don't speak the language. It's all part of the experience. If I drive and do Osmosis Coaching in Austria, it's a different language there, too, and I don't change it up. Not knowing the language forces people to fully open up, and they see the Quality of Life and full integration of life and business in action. They see how I live and understand what we're talking about. The client has dinner with my family and might sit down on my sofa and play with my kids; there's no difference between the client or me.

It's full immersion. And one of our "secret weapons" for accelerated results.

My client sees that when I'm in a meeting, and my kids come in, they have my priority. I say, *"Excuse me for one second,"* talk to them, and redirect them back out. I'm not feeling embarrassed or saying, *"Hey, baby, one second."* That's integration.

Impact Outside of Self-Fulfillment

How do you find impact outside of yourself? What things fulfill you beyond your business or what you do for a living? As you move through this journey towards unleashing your Humble Alpha, you're figuring yourself out. You're filling your cup, elevating your company and everyone you meet, and building strategic partnerships. The next step is finding impact outside of yourself.

How do you really help people in a way that truly aligns with who you are with zero return on investment? How can you help people who can never pay you back in any way, shape, or form?

We're both veterans, and we dedicate part of our time to uplifting and elevating veteran entrepreneurs. You might help the person across the street or get involved in a local charity. If someone in a checkout line at the store doesn't have enough money, you might pay for that person's groceries.

The other day I was in line behind a lady in an electric wheelchair who could only move one hand. She couldn't get her purse and kept dropping it. I was like, *"Ya know, I'm going to do something a little selfish here because I want to get going, so I'm going to pay for her groceries."* Yeah, I had a little return on investment and it was a little selfish, but it was an everyday way for me to pay it forward and make an impact. I also impacted everyone else in line who could now move ahead. You see, there's always a ripple effect.

What you're really doing here is looking for something that you can be a part of that's bigger than yourself. For us, we see the massive guidance needed by military and combat vets who are entrepreneurs. Some of them are stuck; some are just starting out. We love our Vetpreneur Tribe. It's the largest veteran entrepreneur group on Facebook, and we do everything there pro bono. We fund it out of pocket, and it's so fulfilling. The radiant value spreads like wildfire too, because many from the group have started sub-groups. I spend about half an hour a day giving back to this community.

When you impact people, you'll fill up some people's cups who will use that outpouring right up without allowing it to overflow to other people. Make sure that what you choose is in alignment with you. H.I.T. becomes very helpful here because if you set yourself up as a big fish in a little pond, that pond will be drained in no time because you're giving, giving, giving and everyone else is taking, taking, taking. There is no ripple effect. Many people aren't at a place in their lives where they can pour out to others yet, and we understand that. It's okay to pour into those people, but you have to understand (and be okay with) the fact that there won't be an immediate ripple. We do it constantly, but we don't have expectations for a ripple effect.

Give Where More is Given

Let's face it—some charities are so top-heavy they make very little direct impact. For example, March of Dimes is one of the oldest charities in America, but it's called that because only one dime for every dollar goes to charity. The rest goes to administration, fundraising, marketing, etc. Be mindful of who you give your time and money to if you want more money to go directly to more people or causes. Tying it back into partnership alignment, follow the same principles when partnering up with a cause or charity.

As you step into your Humble Alpha, your ability to use your intuition to identify honest, transparent, and aligned people and organizations will skyrocket. When you interact with people or organizations, you'll be able to read them like a book. Just like a book, leave the bad ones half-read on the shelf or in a box, and tell everyone you know about the good ones and how transformative they are.

How to Figure Out Where You Can Make an Impact

Often people don't know where they should give back or focus on making an impact. Look back at one of the biggest challenges you've gone through. It could be a near-death experience or a traumatic situation. That is often the birthplace of your point of impact. You experienced the pain and over-came it. Now, you can comfort and impact someone else experiencing the same thing.

We have a buddy who got his leg blown off in Afghanistan. For a while, it was very depressing for him. He recovered physically, but mentally he struggled. Eventually, he got to a point where he was ready to turn the bad into good and help other people going through what he went through. He started doing that, and he's thriving. He does biking events and triathlons. He's met with former president George W. Bush, and he's living a rich life helping others.

Ask yourself what kind of painful experience you've gone through. How long did it take you to get to the other side? Could you short circuit that pain for someone else? If it took you three years, could you help other people in one year? What injustice do you see that moves or angers you?

Giving Out of a Place of Lack

One of the biggest epidemics we have in the world is that everyone wants to be known as someone who gives or listed as a donor or sponsor. Now that may sound strange that I call it an epidemic, but that's what I believe this is. We see it regularly. People have nothing of their own, and they're giving what they don't have. They don't have abundance; they don't have an over-flowing cup, and they're taking out of the reserves to give to others because of that feeling of significance. It's one of the essential human needs, after all.

You can help someone and feel great, but never have the giving impact you could, because you give from a place of internal lack and exhaustion. I know people who work for the United Nations and live in desolate condi-tions to help people in third-world countries. It's very noble, but some of them have zero internal brightness. They're not giving from an overflowing place within, and it's unhealthy and unbalanced. You can help more people and have more of an impact when you know who you are and are aligned with your purpose

You can take a 50-pound or a 5-pound stone and toss it into the water and make ripples either way. Some form of ripple will be there no matter how much you try to make it more.

When you choose your place of impact, have something to give first. Don't give for the bumper sticker or the significance; give for the ripples. Your impact should be like skipping a stone across a pond and watching the smooth water ripple with the new movement. Yes, the stone should be flat, about the size of the palm of your hand, and about the weight of a tennis ball, but it's all about the grip and motion. We've all seen a person try to skip a rock who doesn't know how to hold it. You can have a stone that meets all of the criteria, but if you don't know how to grip it and toss it, it's going to plunk down to the bottom of the lake rather than ripple across it.

Give of Your Time

If you can't give financially, give of your time. Your discretionary time is one of your most valuable assets. With your time, you can help people come up with strategies or offer wisdom and insight. You can help them make connections and identify opportunities.

When giving of their time, leaders often ask: how do you show others how valuable your time is without asking for money? You don't want to ask for money, but you don't want to get taken advantage of.

This is quite simple. If people want a favor such as an introduction to someone and then go on their merry way, that's one thing. If someone wants you to help them with x,y, and z to have a specific end result, then you need to talk about how that person is going to pay for that. In one instance, you're offering a simple favor, and in another, you're solving one or multiple problems.

If someone comes to you four or five times for help, you say, "Hey, my friend, I love helping you, but what you're taking advantage of is what other people pay for. Let's talk about how we want to move forward." Leaders have a hard time asking for money outside of their jobs or putting a limit on their time. But, it's your time, and you never get it back. It's your time; it's precious. Give it as you see fit, to whom you feel led to give it to, and put a limitation on it when needed.

A Whole Company of Humble Alphas

You're a Humble Alpha. Now it's your turn to help everyone within your organization become Humble Alphas. Your lifestyle, attitude, and confidence are on display, so you're going to reel them in. As you achieve the highest levels of greatness, you can't help but want others to do the same.

If you want to have a team of superstars who appreciate, value, and elevate each other, get them on the Humble Alpha journey. When I led organizations, I talked a lot about relational capital and life enterprise. I made sure everyone knew I was there to invest in them and that I wanted them to have a fantastic Quality of Life at the highest maximum level. I embodied this, and I preached it. They loved Fridays because I would say, *"Hey, as soon as you're done with your goals, you can go home."* Suddenly people would be done in an hour and go home at 10 a.m. Today, they'd hashtag that Quality of Life. When you've become something incredible; you want others to, as well.

Producing from the Inside

When I was in Zurich, Switzerland, leading a team of around 85 people, I implemented the Humble Alpha approach hardcore. When I first stepped in, people wondered who I was, but within a month-and-a-half, I aligned the entire team. The company culture was completely different than it was before. The customers, clients, and members felt the shift. The $100 million investment group that owned it came and asked me what the hell I did. They told me there was no way I could possibly take this team and turn it around so quickly without firing anyone, but I did. We did. It was the power of the Humble Alpha amplified. We produced from the inside out, and led from the internal to the external. They sent me to 50+ locations to replicate it. As a Humble Alpha, you always reproduce because everywhere your foot treads you change the atmosphere. You create space for people to step into their greatness.

Treat people like human beings and ensure they're aligned by ensuring you're aligned. When their talents are aligned, and they see how they fit into the mission, you get the most out of them. You all rise together, but you can't just show people how to rise. You can't just walk in and show the team what to do. You become the Humble Alpha, and through your transformation, you lead them to their own.

Humble Alphas Want to Work with Humble Alphas

A natural byproduct of your becoming a Humble Alpha is that you'll only want to be around other Humble Alphas. Like attracts like. The deals you start doing and the people your company starts to attract will be Humble Alphas. You'll begin to intuitively know when you're aligned with another individual and when you're not.

Intuition is pivotal as a Humble Alpha. I've trained it for years and you have to get used to using it. I'll drive down the road and turn left when my house is to the right simply because my intuition told me to. Intuition shows up for me almost like my breath catching; it takes less than a millisecond.

If I understand it, I act. If I don't understand it at the moment, I pay attention. I push it back down and ask questions: What was the feeling that I had? Was it positive or negative?

Intuition is not a gut feeling; it's an in-between. I don't care what it prompts; I don't second guess it. You do it because you know it's going to lead you to greatness. Intuition separates the superheroes from the winners. The first step is to listen to your intuition, and then the second step is to trust it, and that's a really tough process. Eventually, the trust continues to build until you don't second guess anymore.

Fear is the Door to Greatness

As a Humble Alpha, fear is the door to greatness. There may be times when you want to veer onto a different path, and fear tells you you're leaving money on the table by heading in that direction. Going through the door of fear is like going into a dark basement you haven't been in before. Is Freddy down there? It's scary as hell, but all you have to do is flip the little switch on at the bottom of the stairs and explore what's hidden from the rest of the world or getting dusty because no one realizes they possess a valuable antique treasure.

By applying everything you do at this stage you elevate people to step into the highest version of themselves. Allowing others to address fear as a Humble Alpha and stepping into their greatness. When you do that, you create an entire company of Humble Alphas who perform, innovate, dominate, and have a tremendous Quality of Life. You create a pride that attracts more abundance to your company and impacts the world through their abundance. When a whole company of Humble Alphas™ surrounds you, the world is yours. Heck, it already is.

Before You Continue

As we wrap up this stage (and before you go through the action steps), take a moment and imagine what life will look like when you're filled with true happiness and Quality of Life. What does life look and feel like? How amazing does it feel to know you're fully recharged every single day? How does it feel to know you're making an impact outside of yourself, just because you can? Finally, how does it feel to always be surrounded by other Humble Alphas and those who give back to the world? Grab your bookmark, save this spot, and put this book down. Do this mental exercise and then continue to the action steps.

Action Steps

Wow! You've made it to the end of the final stage in this book! Although these action steps are less "tangible," they may be the most important in the book. Now that you've done all the action steps prior, you have a strong foundation to implement these action steps with full conviction and enthusiasm. Take these steps with just as much intention as the previous stages. Here they are:

1. **Live by H.I.T.** – From this day forward, practice living by H.I.T. Always be honest with yourself and others. It's that simple.

2. **Enjoy the Present Moment** – This is a practice you will cultivate for the rest of your life. Be intentional about enjoying the present moment. Follow the strategies in this book to ensure you cultivate this habit. It will slowly become your new operating system.

3. **Schedule QOL and Recharge** – Ensure you prioritize QOL and Recharge in the following structure in your calendar:

   a. Daily activities for QOL and Recharge

   b. Weekly activities for QOL and Recharge

   c. Monthly activities for QOL and Recharge

   d. Quarterly activities for QOL and Recharge

   e. Annual activities for QOL and Recharge

   f. These are non-negotiable.

4. **Full Integration of Life and Business** – This is more of a mental decision than anything, yet it will continue to impact your

happiness in life. Make the decision now to fully integrate all your life into one.

5. **Identify Impact Outside of Self** – Now that you've gone through the process of this book, this will be much easier to identify. It may still take some time, but you'll know when it's right. Because you have implemented all of the other action steps in this book, your intuition will be strong, and you will trust it. This will help you truly fulfill the human needs for the spirit, specifically contribution.

6. **Grow Humble Alphas™ Within Your Company** – This is the final action step for this book. Your task is to elevate everyone within your company and allow them to step into their version of a Humble Alpha . Because you have gone through this journey, you can become the guide to assist in whatever capacity they need.

Just because this is the last of the action steps in this book, it doesn't mean your work is finished. In fact, it's only begun. The greatness you've pulled out is ever growing and ever increasing. When you compare yourself to 12 months ago, you'll be grateful and surprised by the growth. Twelve months from now, you'll be happily surprised by the growth once again. This will be a continuous cycle. Know that this is the path of growth, and welcome it.

You can download this checklist, along with other worksheets, resources, and videos that help you dig more deeply into these exercises. These bonuses are free of charge, and they come along with this book. To get them go to: HumbleAlphaBook.com/bonus

Conclusion

If you've made it to the end of this book and you want to be a Humble Alpha for ego reasons because you want to be *that* guy, do it! By the time you get to the point in the journey where you start getting results, your ego will begin to disappear. You cannot be egotistical when you're a Humble Alpha. It's impossible because as your life transforms and the way people respond to your shifts, humility and gratitude naturally override the ego.

This doesn't mean it will be easy to keep the ego at bay. In the moments where it rises to the surface, you're challenged and the true Humble Alpha arrives, pulling at your tailcoat through intuition and letting you know you're stepping into the societal trap of having to shout to prove something. We see it often, and it's painfully obvious when someone else is using ego to compensate. It's even more obvious to a Humble Alpha who instinctively knows to elevate the one who compensates. When anyone justifies something through ego, they're seeking significance. As a Humble Alpha, CEO of your own Life Enterprise, and master at creating space and elevating others, you step in to give people exactly what they need to step into their own greatness without ego. This is you, my friend. This is us. This is the Humble Alpha.

If you made it to the end of this book and you feel your Humble Alpha rising to the forefront, take a moment to appreciate it. Most men will never get to this point and fewer men who get to this point will embody these principles and expand upon them so they actually unleash their Humble Alpha everywhere they step for the rest of their lives. The world has tried to put a leash on you, and now you're ripping it off. Keep unleashing.

Acknowledgments

Pat Wenger

Jonathan Hollands

Michael Alois Wagner

Brigadier General (R) Frank Toney

Command Sergeant Major Alton B. Eckert

Command Sergeant Major Jeremy Babcock

Sergeant Major Bobby Norwood

Sergeant Major Michael Bixler

Sergeant First Class Mark Turner

Sergeant Jeffrey Hanson

The Men of ODA 0231

The Men of ODA 0126

Sven von Storch

Beatrix von Storch

Olivia Newton-John

Andrea Bocelli

Veronica Bocelli

Sascha Papadopulos

Geeta Nadkarni

Daryl Hill

Ron Lynch

Jesse Elder

Steve Sims

Tom Matzen

Dan Roitman

Michael Lovitch

Mark Myburgh

Simon Myburgh

Leslie Myburgh

Fabian Chononita

Ollie Jordan Matthews

Joshua B. Lee

Hank Norman

Steve Carlis

Omar Taha

Hayat El Abdelaouie

Mac Lackey

Dwight Sullivan

Chris Voss

Tim Ferriss

Ray Dalio

Tim Storey

Dr. Joe Dispenza

Alan Weiss

Reid Hoffman

Napoleon Hill

James Clear

Michael Neill

Malcolm Gladwell

Wallace D. Wattles

Dr. Joseph Murphy

Joseph Campbell

Gary Vaynerchuk

Donald Miller

Dave Asprey

Robert Greene

Tony Robbins

Cal Newport

Josh Waitzkin

Grant Cardone

Eric Kiker

About The Authors

Steven Kuhn

A Military Combat Veteran, Steven put his experience to work after leaving the military and completing his MBA at Bradford University School of Business Management in Leeds, U.K., by leading teams & turning around multi-million-dollar businesses for twenty plus years in nine countries to the tune of 500 Million+ in revenue. This is the time period when he was involved with some of the world's most famous personalities.

Steven now, along with Lane, wields his talent as a consultant, author and speaker helping leaders "amplify" their Humble Alpha to significantly improve their Quality of Life. This all done through the consistent, conscious application of Honesty, Integrity and Transparency and Investing in Relational Capital, greatly enhancing their life enterprise.

Learn more at: https://humblealphabook.com/bonus

Lane Belone

A Special Forces (Green Beret) veteran, Lane helps entrepreneurs achieve purpose and reach optimal performance. His experience helps him build trust and adaptability as he develops executive teams into laser-focused and empowered "A-Teams".

Learn more at: https://humblealphabook.com/bonus

A Limited Opportunity
For Men Who Seek Greatness:

We are looking for a select few "Humble Alpha's" to join us and are ready to step into their greatness right now.

We will do this together:

- Without cookie-cutter solutions… this will be custom to YOU
- Without preconceived notions… we meet you EXACTLY where you're at right now
- Without pre-recorded trainings… who has time watching hours of videos
- And without complicated systems… just straight to the point

Even after reading this book (that's if you didn't skip to this part of the book without reading the whole thing), implementing the lessons will take time doing it on your own.

If you implement EVERYTHING in this book, there are still two factors that may either hinder your growth or slow it down. What are they?

Blindspots & Shortcuts.

You don't know what you don't know. We even talk about it in the book. Blindspots are incredibly hard to identify without someone who has "been there, done that".

Will you see all your blindspots? Will you even see most of them?

The truth is you'll likely only see a few (if you're lucky).

On the other hand, this entire book is a MASSIVE shortcut to success, fulfillment and Quality of Life. Want to know an even bigger shortcut?

Having custom-tailored, instant feedback on the single most important thing holding you back this very instant. And being able to provide updated shortcuts as you continue to move along gaining presence and impact in your Life Enterprise.

Don't believe us?

Most men don't know how to get rid of the guilt associated with providing money and a great house to your family, but not being able to provide their time (our most precious resource).

We know the answer (it's a shortcut).

Most don't know how to gain true respect for themselves as a man, it's not in the title or position they hold. [Insert powerful CEO who everyone respects at work, but don't respect him as a man]

We know the answer (another shortcut).

Most don't know how to eliminate the overwhelm with the pressure to perform at work and provide for their family. [Men live with this problem for years, even DECADES. We wouldn't call it living.]

We know the answer (indeed a shortcut).

Even with all this, do you want to know the worst part of it all?

No one has the guts to tell you the truth.

Actually two truths. The truth in what you're actually not dealing with that is causing you frustration, overwhelm and stress. And the truth on how to get out of it.

We tell you the truth.

So with all this said, what's the deal?

You now know the power of this book and how it will help you step into your greatness. What you don't know is how long it all will take when you do it on your own.

Simply put: Identifying blindspots and applying shortcuts will rapidly collapse time to get you exactly where you want to be.

Who is the ideal fit?

- You're ready to fully decide on yourself and finally reject the premise "I'm doing good enough".
- Your ready to shift focus on success in life first, because then success in business is a given.
- You believe there must be a "better" paradigm for living compared to how you currently live.
- You have the resources to invest in yourself and make this happen now because you know it's time.
- You're not afraid to step into the unknown of life and absolutely crush it.

Does all that describe you?
To learn more visit https://www.HumbleAlpha.com/greatness

Personality
Introvert, enquiring, calming, steady, accountable, generous, inclusive,

Mind
Learning, growth,

Body

Printed in Great Britain
by Amazon

59514346R00118